PROPHECY AND POLITICS

PROPHECY AND POLITICS

The Secret Alliance Between Israel and the U.S. Christian Right

Grace Halsell

LAWRENCE HILL BOOKS

*Lawrence Hill Books is an imprint of
Chicago Review Press, Incorporated
814 North Franklin Street
Chicago, Illinois 60610*

Library of Congress Cataloging-in-Publication Data

Halsell, Grace.
  Prophecy and politics.

  Includes index.
  1. Fundamentalism—History of doctrines—20th century.
2. Christian Zionism—History of doctrines—20th century.
3. End of the world. 4. Falwell, Jerry. 5. United States—
Politics and government—1981. 6. United States—Military
relations—Israel. 7. Israel—Military relations—United
States. I. Title.
BT82.2.H35 1986   280'.4   86-12102
ISBN 1-55652-054-9

10 9 8 7 6 5 4 3 2 1

Printed in the United States of America

To those who seek peace

Contents

EXPLORING NON-JEWISH ZIONISM

PROPHECY AND POLITICS

Prologue

I grew up in a small, windblown town on the high, dry plains of West Texas. It was said that out there one could look farther—and see less than almost anywhere.

I was carried in my mother's or father's arms to church, twice on Sundays, and to Wednesday night prayer meetings. Absorbing biblical terms and concepts as part of my thought process, I was indoctrinated into fundamentalist Christianity as effortlessly as breathing the clear, dry Texas air. The word of God, I was taught, comes to us through the Bible, free of all mistakes in translations and free of all typographical errors. Every "i" has been dotted and every "t" crossed. I heard repeatedly that the Bible is inerrant, infallible. As a child, I did not know the meaning of the words but they became lodged deep in my memory.

One summer, when I was nine, I visited my maternal grandparents in Arlington, Texas. Located between Dallas and Fort Worth, Arlington in that era was a quiet village of so few people everyone knew everyone else.

A "great revivalist"—as my Grandmother Shanks identified a peripatetic preacher otherwise known as Brother Turner—came to town, put up his tent and preached for a week. Grandmother and I attended every night. Brother Turner preached fire-and-brimstone sermons, telling us that the world is divided into the wicked and the good, the wicked doomed for hell and only the born-again Christians escaping everlasting fire. "Repent or perish!" he warned.

All of us listening to him were spellbound. Having no radio, television or public cultural events, we depended to a great extent on revivalists such as Brother Turner to bring us knowledge and understanding.

5

Each night, I experienced a sense of excitement, growing anticipation. Then came the final night of the revival. Brother Turner held a large Bible in his left hand, quoted directly from God and in conclusion asked those who had not confessed Christ publicly to come forward. Mrs. Triplett, who played the piano, struck the notes for the well-known hymn, "Just As I Am."

We stood to sing. Grandmother and I held a hymnal, but we knew the words by heart:

> Just as I am/without one plea
> But that thy blood/was shed for me
> And that thou bidst me/come to Thee
> Oh Lamb of God, I come
> I come . . .

No one came forward. Brother Turner asked us to be seated. And he asked Mrs. Triplett to continue playing while we all bowed our heads. After asking those who knew they were saved to raise their hands, he called on those who had not raised their hands to come forward and be saved.

Everyone seemed to be thinking of me in those moments. Everyone was softly singing:

> Just as I am/and waiting not
> To rid my soul/of one dark blot . . .

Suddenly, as if propelled by forces outside myself, I rose from the wooden bench and moved forward, alone, to where the evangelist was standing. He put his arms around me. And soon my grandmother, neighbors and friends were there to embrace me. I felt myself shaking uncontrollably. Tears were streaming down my face.

Grandmother wrote my parents that I had been saved. And at summer's end, I returned to Lubbock.

In Lubbock, in the years I was growing up, being saved was a prime topic of conversation. It was not considered unusual for a man, like my father, to encounter a stranger and without preliminary words of salutation ask, "Are you a Christian? Are you saved?"

Born-again Christians in my town believed that human history as we know it will end in a battle called Armageddon and culminate with the return of Christ, who on His return will pass final judgment on all the living as well as the dead.

Generally, the Christians of the town also believed:

The world was about 6,000 years old.

Mary, the mother of Jesus, was a virgin.

The Jews are God's Chosen People.

God gave the Holy Land to His Chosen People, the Jews.

Because the Jews are His Chosen People, God blesses those who bless the Jews and curses those who curse the Jews.

In Sunday School, I studied a book with colored pictures of faraway places and bearded men wearing flowing robes. I listened to Old Testament stories of the Hebrews' sojourn in Palestine.

Early on, I had a desire to become a sojourner, too. When I was 19, I left Lubbock, my family and security. Earning my living as a writer, I lived for years at a stretch in Europe, Korea, Japan and South America. And eventually, I went to Vietnam as a reporter. I saw hospitals filled with women and children without arms or legs—victims of U.S.-made bombs that were dropped from American planes. Many victims, pointing to the sky, spoke these words in English: "Fire! American fire!"

Why, I wondered, were we killing Vietnamese?

Leaving Vietnam, I returned to the United States and settled in Washington, D.C., where I was a reporter, covering the presidency of Lyndon B. Johnson. One day President Johnson personally hired me to work for him as a White House staff writer.

He continued to escalate the war, sending more American soldiers to kill and be killed. Often I saw him agonize over the killings. "I was up all night," he would say. He felt himself trapped. His ego trapped him—his indoctrination that strong men win battles.

Why, I kept asking, do we not see Vietnamese as people? How can I say to President Johnson and others, They are real—as real as you and me? Then I asked myself, Were there other groups of people we did not see? As a white, growing up in Texas, I had never really seen black people. Was their being invisible the racism within me? To explore that question, I left my White House job. After darkening my skin, I lived as a black woman and recorded my experiences in a book. Later I learned about the life of an Indian woman while living on the Navajo reservation in New Mexico and Arizona. Still later, I experienced life as a Mexican wetback who crosses the U.S.-Mexico borders without documents.

Eventually, I went to the Middle East. Before going there, I had not studied the culture and history of the area to any great extent. Rather, my knowledge of the Middle East came almost exclusively from the Bible. In this respect, I was typical of many Americans.

In 1979, in occupied Palestine, I met for the first time a Palestinian. He told how he had been forced, at gunpoint, to leave the land farmed by his father's father's father—back as far as memory served.

I stayed in one of the illegal West Bank Jewish settlements called Tekoa. I lived awhile in the home of Linda and Bobby Brown, third-generation Americans who told me they had used rifles and Uzi submachine guns to take land from Palestinian farmers.

"God gave this land to us—the Jews," Bobby Brown of Brooklyn said.

Suddenly all that I had been taught as a child flashed back to me. God had a Chosen People. And God gave the Holy Land to His Chosen People.

Now I was in the Holy Land. It was not Brother Turner speaking the words—back in the days when there was no political entity called Israel on our maps. It was a man from Brooklyn. And the land on which we sat was not mystical, other-worldly biblical Zion, but the land—and the livelihood—of Palestinians who had lived there for the past 2,000 years.

In that moment I came face to face with a very important question that had been with me since childhood. Did God indeed have favorite people? A second question came to mind: How could a modern state called Israel be identified with ancient, biblical and mystical Zion?

After initial visits to the Holy Land, I wanted to investigate further my own belief system regarding Christianity and to learn what others thought regarding the End of Time. I read *The Late Great Planet Earth,* which reportedly has sold an estimated 18 million copies. It was a best-seller all during the 1970s, outselling any other book except the Bible. In this and four other books, including *There's a New World Coming,* author Hal Lindsey declares God has foreordained that we fight a nuclear Armageddon.

Lindsey tells us that we must pass through seven time periods, or dispensations—one of which includes the terrible battle of Armageddon, where new and totally destructive nuclear weapons will be unleashed. Because the prescribed time periods are called dispensations, the belief system itself is known as dispensationalism, while the believers in this system are called dispensationalists.

Dispensationalism spread in the United States largely through the efforts of Cyrus Ingerson Scofield. Scofield, the author of the *Scofield Reference Bible,* which sells in the multi-millions of copies, taught that born-again Christians should welcome Armageddon, because once the fighting began the "saved" would be lifted up into the clouds in what is called the Rapture.

In 1980, I began listening to popular U.S. television ministers, who according to a 1985 Nielsen survey reach an estimated 60 million listeners. They are convincing millions of Christian listeners that they should not work for peace, but rather accept war as the will of God. They say God has foreordained from the beginning of time that precisely those of us living in this generation must wage a nuclear war.

The ministers quote scripture, often from Ezekiel, Daniel, or Revelation, to "prove" that we are in "the last days." They tend to ignore the Sermon on the Mount. Nor do they remind us that Christ possessed a way that was not based on military strength, that he came with a message of peace.

The belief system of those who preach Armageddon theology centers around the biblical land of Zion and the modern

Zionist state of Israel, which they equate as one and the same. Because they believe it is necessary for Israel to be the "landing base" for the Second Coming of Christ, they tend to make a cult of the land of Israel.

Most American TV evangelists, along with writer Hal Lindsey, repeat the same message: this planet Earth will very likely in our lifetime become "the late great planet Earth." God knows it will happen; He knew it from the very beginning. God kept his plan secret from all the billions of people who lived before us, but now he has revealed the plan to Lindsey and others, such as Jerry Falwell, Jimmy Swaggart, and Pat Robertson, who preach Armageddon theology.

On December 2, 1982, I listened to Jerry Falwell say that the word Armageddon "strikes fear into the hearts of people." He concluded his sermon by giving his audience a big smile and saying, "Hey, it's great being a Christian! We have a wonderful future ahead." His theology of course relegates all who are not born again to eternal damnation.

Speaking on June 9, 1982 to listeners of the Christian Broadcasting Network's *700 Club,* Pat Robertson said: "This whole thing (the battle of Armageddon) is now in place. It can happen any time (to) fulfill Ezekiel. It is ready to happen . . . the United States is in that Ezekiel passage, and . . . we are standing by."

In Armageddon theology the message is plain: war is inevitable, so let's get on with it. All of this looms important in view of the political implications of a dispensationalist in the U.S. presidential office. While Robertson did not secure the 1988 Republican nomination for president, he and millions of loyal followers exert a strong influence on the Republican party. And there is always the danger that strong advocates of Armageddon theology may influence politicians to adopt comparable apocalyptic views. James Watt is an example. As Interior Secretary he indicated to a U.S. House of Representatives committee that, in view of Christ's imminent return, he couldn't worry much about the destruction of our natural resources.

The dangerous message that Armageddon must-come-to-destroy planet Earth is not of course confined within the borders of the United States. The advocates of this scenario operate internationally, from a base headquarters in Jerusalem that they call the International Christian Embassy. In August 1985, this group staged what was termed the first Christian Zionist Congress. As part of my research into Christian Zionism, I attended the Congress as one of 589 persons from 27 countries. We met in sessions held in the same hall where eighty-eight years earlier Theodor Herzl had called delegates to the first Jewish Zionist Congress. Herzl, known as the father of political Jewish Zionism, made an appeal for Jews to live exclusively among Jews. He said all the world hated Jews, and that they could be safe only among themselves.

At the Congress I listened for three days to Christian speakers review the horrors of the Nazi holocaust against the Jews. No speaker, Israeli Jew or Christian, suggested that in a nuclear age all human beings must somehow learn to live as good neighbors. Rather than offer hope by suggesting steps whereby Jews and Arabs might reach reconciliation and peace, each speaker seemed to reinforce the Jews' haunting fears about security. Rather than stressing how much Arabs and Jews, and indeed all human beings, have in common, the speakers told us: Jews are different. They must live exclusively among Jews.

The Christians proposed a resolution urging Israel to annex the West Bank, with its nearly one million Palestinians. An Israeli Jew, seated in the audience, rose before the motion was voted upon to suggest that the language be modified. He pointed out that an Israeli poll showed that one-third of the Israelis would be willing to trade territory seized in 1967 for peace with the Palestinians. In answer to this, one Christian leader shouted: "We don't care what the Israelis vote! We care what God says! And God gave the land to the Jews!" The Christians then passed the resolution.

As part of my research into Armageddon theology, I also made two trips to the Holy Land that were sponsored by Jerry Falwell. I was one of 630 Christians on a 1983 trip and one of 850 on a 1985 trip. Falwell did not himself accompany the groups. However, in each instance he flew over to Israel for the last three days of the tour. In 1983, he gave a banquet honoring then Defense Minister Moshe Arens. At this banquet I heard Falwell thank Arens for a Windstream jet that the Israelis had given to him. On the 1985 trip, Falwell gave a banquet honoring Ariel Sharon, the mastermind of the Israeli invasion of Lebanon that killed and wounded 200,000 persons, most of them civilians. Falwell called Sharon one of the greatest of men, in the same category, he said, "as George Washington and Abraham Lincoln."

Falwell, his assistants, and our Israeli guides generally ignored the Palestinians—Christians and Muslims alike. When they were mentioned, they were represented as obstacles to God's will as it was being carried out by the likes of Begin, Arens, Sharon, and Shamir.

In 1985, Dr. John Walvoord of the Dallas Texas Theological Seminar, a seedbed for Armageddon theology, spoke to Falwell's group of pilgrims in Jerusalem. He told us that the Jews are God's chosen people. In a personal interview, I asked him about the injustices suffered by the Palestinians that I had witnessed. "Frankly," he told me, "God didn't have them in His master plan. His concern was for the Jews, to whom He had given the Holy Land."

If one accepts the premise that there is a chosen people and a chosen land—and that a biblical, allegorical, spiritual Zion is indeed one and the same as a modern, political, Zionist entity—then one does not criticize Israel as one might criticize Ireland, England, France, Germany, or the United States. Even the politics and the wars of the chosen land become "holy."

Since Christian Zionists believe that God is personally involved in all actions taken by the Israelis, they easily concede that others, in particular the United States, should give Israel whatever it wants, whether this be U.S. planes to bomb an Iraqi nuclear facility, jets to bomb Libya, or American negotiations with a "moderate" Iranian, Manucher Ghorbanifar, who in reality was acting as an agent for the Israelis.

When Ghorbanifar offered to transfer to the Contras some of the vast profits made on arms sales to Iran, Lieutenant Colonel Oliver North said he assumed the offer was made "with the full knowledge, acquiescence, and support, if not the original idea, of the Israeli intelligence services, if not the Israeli government." In his testimony before the U.S. Select Committee on July 8, 1987, North also said that he and the director of the CIA were aware that Israel was playing a double game with them. But because they were Israelis, the American officials accepted the deceit.

North, a born-again charismatic—one who believes in faith healing and the "power" of speaking in tongues—was putty in the hands of the Zionists. He so endeared himself to them that one Israeli general, Uri Simhoni, observed, "Do you know why we get along with him so well? It's because he is more of an Israeli than we Israelis."

The danger of Christian Zionists such as North making U.S. policies lies in the fact that they believe God is always on Israel's side. The task of educating U.S. Christians on Middle East issues—and, I will add, Christ's true mission of peace—is a large one. Increasingly, as our problems of broken homes, bad economic news, and drugs loom larger, many Christians find it comfortable to accept the idea that everything is in God's hands, including the issue of war and peace. Americans now listen to over 1,400 religious stations. Of the 80,000 fundamentalist pastors who broadcast daily over 400 radio stations, a vast majority are dispensationalists. They give their audiences answers and a certitude that God will protect them.

Meanwhile, the certitude of some was shaken in 1987 and 1988—banner years of scandal for American TV evangelists. Many thought it was a scandal that Pat Robertson claimed to be a Korea "combat veteran." And that Oral Roberts begged for $8 million to save him from his killer god. Or that Tammy Bakker was on drugs, Jim Bakker had committed adultery, and that Falwell in a "diabolical plot" allegedly seized the Bakkers' $172 million PTL television empire. Meanwhile, Jimmy Swaggart, who spoke regularly to audiences of four and one-half million viewers, admitted that he had a "fascination" for pornography and visited prostitutes.

But even though these scandals gained headlines, they were minor offenses, compared with a deeper, more persistent scandal that lies in the realm of global politics concerning the survival of humankind and our planet Earth. The media scarcely touches this major scandal, involving the political dimensions of TV evangelists who convince millions of their followers that God wants us to end the world.

The 1985 Nielsen survey mentioned earlier shows that 40 percent of all American viewers regularly listen to preachers who tell them we can do nothing to prevent a nuclear war in our lifetime. According to this survey, some of the most popular TV evangelists who preach Armageddon theology include:

• Pat Robertson, who hosts a fast-paced, 90-minute daily talk show called the *700 Club* (named for his original 700 contributors). He reaches more than 16 million families (or, as the poll puts it, television households). That's slightly more than 19 percent of all Americans who own TV sets.

Robertson, the son of the late U.S. Senator Willis Robertson of Virginia and a graduate of Yale University Law School and New York Theological Seminary, employs about 1,300 people to run his Christian Broadcasting Network Corporation (CBN), with headquarters in a $22 million International Communications Center on 679 acres in suburban Virginia Beach. CBN includes the *700 Club,* three television stations, a radio station, the CBN cable channel, a television station in southern Lebanon, international broadcasts in more than 60 countries, a university, a worldwide charity system and a lobbying group. Robertson's operations bring in an estimated $200 million a year.

• Although he was defrocked by leaders of the Assemblies of God, Jimmy Swaggart, who operates out of Baton Rouge, Louisiana, is still a popular TV evangelist. In 1985, he reached a total of four and one-half million households daily (or 5.4 percent of all viewers) and a total of nine and one-quarter million households (or 10.9 percent of all viewers) on Sundays.

• Jim Bakker began his religious career under the tutelage of Pat Robertson. Until his admitted sexual tryst with Jessica

Hahn, he was reaching nearly six million households daily, or 6.8 percent of all viewers.

With a home base in Charlotte, North Carolina, Bakker and his wife Tammy owned a $449,000 mountainside home in Palm Desert, California, along with a Rolls-Royce and a Mercedes-Benz. His PTL (Praise the Lord) "inspirational network" was carried on 825 cable systems and was the nation's nineteenth largest cable network. Bakker's enterprises earned an estimated $50 million to $100 million a year.

• Oral Roberts, whose TV programs reach 5.77 million households (6.8 percent of all viewers), was born in a log house in Oklahoma in 1918, the son of a farmer turned Pentecostal preacher. Oral Roberts says God told him to found his university. God told him, in 1968, to leave the Pentecostal Holiness Church and become a Methodist minister. In 1977, after he lost his daughter and son-in-law in a plane crash, Roberts said God inspired him to build the City of Faith hospital. He is one of two Americans who have singlehandedly built a university, medical school and hospital. (The other was Johns Hopkins.)

• Jerry Falwell with his *Old Time Gospel Hour* each week goes into 5.6 million households (6.6 percent of all viewers).

In 1985, Falwell, like Robertson, was deeply involved in politics. In August, after he spent five days in South Africa, Falwell voiced support for the apartheid government and called Nobel peace laureate Bishop Desmond Tutu a "phony." The Tutu remark, according to a September 25 Associated Press story, caused contributions to Falwell to fall $1 million below anticipated levels.

Undaunted, Falwell traveled in November, 1985 to Manila, where he voiced support for the Marcos dictatorship and called the strife-torn Philippines "a paradise." On January 25, 1986, Falwell hosted a luncheon in Washington, D.C., honoring then Vice President George Bush. Falwell told 500 persons—who were treated to a well-planned, lavish, and all-for-free luncheon—that Bush would make the best president in 1988.

• Kenneth Copeland reaches 4.9 million households (5.8 percent of all viewers) each week. A graduate of Oral Roberts University, he is also a dispensationalist who sees modern Israel as the same as biblical Zion:

"God has raised up Israel . . . We're watching Him move in behalf of Israel . . . What an excellent time to begin to support our government as it supports Israel . . . What an excellent time . . . to let God know how much you appreciate the very roots of Abraham." Despite such testimonies of devotion, dispensationalists such as Copeland do not necessarily love or even like Israel *per se*. Rather they express a love for Israel because they perceive it as providing the site for the battle of Armageddon and the return of Christ. And they express a love for the Jews not because they are Jews, but rather because they perceive them as stellar actors on the stage unfolding the time periods or dispensations that they, the dispensationalists, need for their own Christian expectations.

TV ratings in late 1988 show that Copeland's popularity is steadily increasing. His Armageddon theology has an ever-growing audience.

• Richard De Haan with his *Day of Discovery* reaches 4.075 million households (4.8 percent of all viewers). He is the son of M. R. De Haan of Grand Rapids, Michigan, who in his lifetime promoted dispensationalism perhaps more than any other American minister.

I list only seven religious broadcasters of the many thousands who preach Armageddon theology on radio, TV and from the pulpit. Of the 4,000 evangelical-fundamentalists who annually attend the National Religious Broadcasters Convention, an estimated 3,000 are dispensationalists who believe that only a nuclear holocaust can bring Christ back to earth.

Because of the scandals, the popularity of a few of the religious TV stars such as Swaggart and Bakker has plunged. "But this is a temporary set-back," states Jeffrey Hadden of the University of Virginia, and an authority on the subject of TV evangelists. "In terms of long-term trends, they will regain their popularity—while others, like Copeland, are steadily attracting more viewers. And new 'stars' are appearing with equal charismatic appeal." Because all the symptoms of our society which made the militant TV evangelists popular in the first place are still evident, Hadden sees no long-range decline in their magnetic appeal.

Meanwhile, the voices for war seem to be on the rise. Most Bible schools across America—denominational and non-denominational—teach dispensationalism and Armageddon theology based on a cult of Israel. Dale Crowley, Jr., a Washington, D.C.-based minister whose father, Dale Crowley, Sr., was a founding member of the National Religious Broadcasters told me: "Schools such as the Moody Bible Institute of Chicago, the Philadelphia College of the Bible, the Bible Institute of Los Angeles, and about two hundred others are turning out students steeped in Scofieldism—in dispensationalism and a cult of Israel. Eighty to ninety percent of the teachers and students study Scofield and believe in a Rapture and nuclear Armageddon. There are now about 100,000 students in these Bible schools. And they will go out into the world and become ministers and preach this doctrine, or they will start their own Bible schools and teach it."

Learning about militant, muscular Christians who preach about an inevitable nuclear war can serve one purpose for peace-minded men and women: it will make clear that the task before us is not an easy one. And that millions of "well-meaning" Christians are part of the problem. Rather than remaining silent on this issue, all peace-minded people can best prevent a nuclear Armageddon by speaking out against the alliance between the state of Israel and the militant members of the U.S. Christian right.

Grace Halsell
Washington, D.C.
March 1989

WITH
JERRY FALWELL
IN THE LAND OF CHRIST

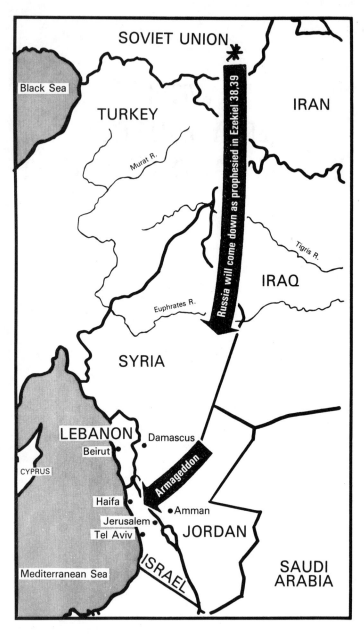

Maps such as this are distributed by some fundamentalist groups

The Battle
of Armageddon

Starting in 1980, I made a habit of tuning into Jerry Falwell's Old Time Gospel Hour each Sunday on TV.

To learn more about Falwell's Armageddon theology, and to know to what extent his followers think as he does, I signed to go on a 1983 Jerry Falwell-sponsored tour of the Holy Land.

I was one of 630 Christians who flew out of New York to Tel Aviv, where we were divided into groups of about 50. Each of us was assigned to a certain bus, with a designated Israeli guide. After an overnight rest in Tel Aviv, we were on our buses.

Now, go with me on a short journey:

To get to Megiddo, we travel north from Tel Aviv for 55 miles. We arrive at a site that lies 20 miles south-southeast of Haifa and about 15 miles inland from the Mediterranean Sea. On leaving the bus, my steps fall in with Clyde, a retired Minneapolis business executive who is in his late 60s. Clyde, a college graduate, had served as an Army captain in North Africa and Europe during World War II and had been honored for his intelligent command of soldiers and his personal courage under fire. He stands six feet tall, with good posture, which he credits to his service in the army.

Clyde's wife died two years ago, and he later decided to take this trip on his own. He is dressed neatly, with worsted wool trousers, white shirt, subdued tie and a cashmere jacket. He has a full head of hair, only partially gray.

We walk a short distance to a tell, or mound—an artificial hill covering the successive layers of remains of ancient communities.

"An old Canaanite city once was here," Clyde remarks, adding that we are on the southern rim of the large flat expanse of the plain of Esdraelon, also called in Scripture the valley of Jezreel.

"In ancient times, Megiddo was a city of great importance. It lay at the strategic crossing of important military and caravan routes," Clyde, a history buff, says. "The Via Maris, the old coastal route linking Egypt with Damascus and the East, traversed this valley by Megiddo."

So, I suggest, this site has always been a battlefield?

"Yes," Clyde agrees. "Some historians believe that more battles have been fought here than at any other place in the world. Ancient conquerors used to say that any leader who held Megiddo could withstand all invaders.

"You read in Joshua 12:21 how Joshua and the Israelites defeated the Canaanites here in one battle. And two centuries later the Israelite forces under Deborah and Barak—read in Judges 4 and 5—won a battle against the Canaanite captain Sisera.

"And then, as we know, King Solomon fortified the city, making it into a military center for his horses and chariots.

"Even in my lifetime, we've had important battles here. Near the end of World War I, in 1918, the British General Allenby won a crucial victory over the Turks right here at Megiddo."

All the members of our party continue walking to a vantage point, and then we stop to absorb a commanding view of the valley of Jezreel stretching out to the northwest far into the distance.

"At last!" Clyde remarks in a voice filled with emotion, "I am viewing the site of the last great battle!"

But how, I ask, did he know a final battle would be waged here?

"You take the name—Megiddo—and add the additional Hebrew word *har*, meaning mountain, and that gives you a phrase meaning the mountain of Megiddo or 'Har-Megiddo.' That translates into the word Armageddon."

As he speaks, I try to follow his reasoning by looking for the *har*, or mountain, but I do not find it. Since I see the valley before us, however, I reason that the vantage point on which we stand can easily be considered the *har*. Even so, would not Har-Megiddo—literally the mountain of Megiddo—mean a place, not an event?

"No, no," Clyde replies, somewhat impatient. "This is the site of the battle involving all nations. It will be the final battle between the forces of good, led by Christ, and the forces of evil, led by the Antichrist."

Like millions of others, I admit to Clyde, I have always heard of Armageddon. But while often hearing the word, I did not know its derivation. Had Clyde, I ask, read much about Armageddon?

"You know we find the word Armageddon only once in the Bible. That, of course, is in the Book of Revelation. That's chapter 16, verse 16." And Clyde quotes the short verse:

"And he gathered them together into a place called in the Hebrew tongue Armageddon."

Since this word Armageddon looms so important in our lives, I hope to pin down its derivation. I repeat what Clyde has said: the Old Testament makes no mention of the word. And the New Testament mentions the word only in one instance, in Revelation, sometimes called the Apocalypse or the Revelation of St. John. Still, I am confused. Whereas Revelation speaks of "a place" called Armageddon, Clyde insists that Armageddon means a battle.

"John the Divine wrote the book of Revelation," Clyde says. "And as you know it's from John that we get most of our information on these final days we are passing through. He gives us a perfect picture of this last battle to be fought right here. You recall that in his vision of that great battle he wrote: 'The cities of the nation fell . . . and every island fled away and the mountains were not found.' " Clyde then adds:

"God knows everything about the future—nothing escapes Him. God knew from the beginning who would go to hell and precisely who would not. When God gave the law, He knew that man was incapable of keeping it."

I venture to ask:

He foreknows—and He has foreordained?

"You've got to remember foreknowing does not predetermine everything. But what God knows He knows beyond all guessing. What God knows He knows 100 percent. And He knows everything.

"In the Book of Revelation, God uses John to give us a good description of what this last battle will be like," Clyde continues. "A 200-million- man Oriental army will be moving westward for one year. This army will move through and destroy the most populated area of the world before arriving at the River Euphrates.

"Revelation 16 tells us that the River Euphrates will be dry and this will permit the kings of the East, the Orientals, to cross into Israel."

The *kings* of the East?—I repeat. My mind flits to the area of the world east of the Euphrates. I can call to mind no kings in that area of the world today. In our time, the shah of Iran was the last king east of the Euphrates. There being no kings today—there were kings in John's time—would it not indicate, I suggest, that John was writing for his own age, not ours?

"No, no—" says Clyde. "You can take 'kings' to mean leaders, heads of state." A literalist, Clyde, in this instance does not take the Bible literally. I do not interrupt, and Clyde continues his narrative: "The kings—or leaders—will move the greatest army in the history of the world right here to Megiddo." His eyes enlarge and his face takes on a glow of anticipation as he talks of an angel pouring out a vial upon the great river Euphrates and the water drying up, permitting the vast army to march across the riverbed.

But how, when it is so difficult to organize one good army, much less all the armies of the Orient, could one man do this? Or one group of leaders?

"Oh, that's clear," says Clyde. "The leaders have geopolitical goals, but they are motivated by 'demonic spirits.' "

Demonic spirits? I ask.

"In this case, they are the demonic spirits of the fallen angels who followed Lucifer in his rebellion against God. After these demonic spirits gain control of the minds of the world leaders, these leaders and the armies of the world unknowingly become their pawns."

I seem to be fitting it all together. To make sure I am on the right track, I suggest that it will be the Antichrist who puts the demonic spirits into the leaders of the world, and Clyde says that is right.

Besides the demonic spirits, Clyde talks of the "beast" of John's Revelation, explaining that "the beast means there will be a powerful union of ten European nations or groups of nations that will arise in the last days. Now we know we are living in the last days because we have seen the rise of that union of powerful European nations—that's what we call the European Economic Community or the Common Market. By studying prophecy, one can see that God has foretold all of these developments.

"Everything we read that's happening in the world today indicates clearly that this battle will take place very soon.

"And in this final battle—you learn this from studying Zechariah as well as Revelation—the forces of the nations of the entire earth under the Antichrist will be fighting against King Jesus and his glorified saints. And as we know, Christ, in history's bloodiest battle, will devastate millions and destroy the Antichrist."

To prove his point, Clyde quotes from memory Second Thessalonians 2:8:

"And then shall that Wicked"—which means, Clyde adds, the lawless one, or the Antichrist—"be revealed, whom the Lord shall consume with the spirit of His mouth, and shall destroy with the brightness of His coming."

It is unlikely, I comment to Clyde, that Christians have devoted more thoughts and words to any other place—outside heaven and hell—than to the idea of an Armageddon.

As Clyde and I stand talking, others in our group take seats on rocks or on the grass, contemplating the valley with its patchwork fields of wheat, barley and fruit orchards. While it looks so quiet, so peaceful, Clyde's demeanor and words make the world going up in a big bang appear inevitable. He seems certain of his details and figures regarding the final conflagration.

Yet this battle is to be waged in a field before us—a valley so small it would fit into a Nebraska farm and be lost if placed in a big Texas ranch. Gesturing toward the minuscule quiet valley of terraced fields, I remark to Clyde that it looks very small for the last, great decisive battle.

"No," he says, quite serious. "You can get a lot of tanks in here."

Tanks, I repeat, and all the armies of the earth?

"All of this. But you've got to remember this will be the greatest battle ever fought. Several million will die right here."

And a nuclear war will start here at Megiddo, and destroy the world? I ask.

"Yes," he replies. "You read this in Ezekiel, chapters 38 and 39. It describes a nuclear war, saying there will be 'torrential rains and hailstone, fire and brimstone' and 'a great shaking in the land' with mountains falling and cliffs collapsing and walls tumbling to the ground in the face of 'every kind of terror.' Ezekiel could scarcely have been referring to anything other than an exchange of tactical nuclear weapons."

Clyde's certitude staggers my sense of reality. Yet I know that he speaks what literally millions of Americans believe.

And did Clyde, I ask, visualize Christ, rather like a five-star general leading an army? And does he interpret Scripture to say that Jesus as Supreme Commander will destroy forces allied against Him by the use of nuclear weapons?

"Yes," he responds. "In fact, we can expect that Christ will make the first strike. He will release a new weapon. And this weapon will have the same effects as those caused by a neutron bomb. You read in Zechariah 14:12, that 'their flesh shall consume away while they stand upon their feet and their eyes shall consume away in their holes, and their tongue shall consume away in their mouth.' "

But is Clyde saying Christ Himself will make the first strike? Before replying, Clyde draws himself up to his full six feet:

"Yes, Jesus Christ returns to this earth to restore the government of God and to bring world peace. And He will take command of the world. And do so from His headquarters in Jerusalem," Clyde tells me in a strong, deadly earnest voice.

And what about the Jewish people living in Israel?

"Two-thirds of all the Jews living here will be killed," Clyde says. "You read that in Zechariah 13:8-9. There are about 13 and a half million Jews in the world today. So God is telling us that nine million Jews will be killed in this battle—more than all the Jews killed by the Nazis. So much blood will flow that God likens it to a wine press that presses out blood. For 200 miles the blood will reach up to the horses' bridles!"

Why, I ask, did Clyde suppose God wanted to pour out a series of judgments that would kill most of the world's people and destroy most of our civilization?

"He's doing it mainly for his ancient people, the Jews," Clyde replies. "He devised a seven-year Tribulation period mainly to purge the Jews, to get them to see the light and recognize Christ as their savior."

I confess his interpretation is confusing to me. Why would God have chosen the Jews, his favorite among all the world's people, only to exterminate most of them—in Clyde's euphemistic word, to "purge" them?

"Don't you see? God wants them to bow down before His only son, who is our Lord Jesus Christ."

Then Clyde explains that after having exterminated two-thirds of the people, God would save the Land of Israel—that He Himself would enter into the battle of Armageddon. "And He has all He needs to destroy those who are determined to harm Israel." It begins to sound to me as if Clyde loves Israel but does not especially like the Jews. He seems to have little or no remorse for the Jews and others he says would be killed.

"It will take the Jews living in Israel seven months to bury all the dead soldiers." As proof, Clyde quotes Ezekiel 39:12: "And seven months shall the house of Israel be burying of them, that they may cleanse the land."

At the risk of repeating myself, I again ask why a God of mercy would want us to use nuclear weapons?

"Remember," he replies, "man obtained from God his knowledge of how to create destructive power. Nuclear energy is not new to God. And the threat of a nuclear holocaust does not take Him by surprise. At all times God knows how many fish are in the sea, how many stars are in the sky and how many grains of sand are on the seashore. He is sovereign, supreme in power. What He decides must take place. No man or nation can prevent what He wills from occurring.

"When Christ comes to earth again, he will descend out of the skies over Jerusalem. You see, all history has in a sense been predetermined by God. And all history relates and is centered on this nation of Israel, which is the apple of God's eye. So, in the great final battle God will again take charge of human history," Clyde concludes, giving me an enigmatic smile.

"The End is Near"

On the Holy Land tour, I had tape-recorded Clyde's words and later when I listened to them, they sounded very much the same as what Jerry Falwell and most major TV evangelists say: we are moving inexorably toward a nuclear holocaust. The script has already been written. As Clyde put it, God is taking charge of human history.

On my return from the 1983 trip, I investigated what other evangelical-fundamentalists had said on the subject of Armageddon. In 1970, Billy Graham warned that the world is "moving now very rapidly toward its Armageddon" and "the present generation of young people may be the last generation in history."

"Now many people ask where is Armageddon, how close are we to it?" Graham said on another occasion. "Well, it's west of the Jordan, between Galilee and Samaria in the plain of Jezreel. And Napoleon saw that great place one time and he said, 'This would make the greatest battlefield in the world.' For the Bible teaches that the last great war of history will be fought in that part of the world: the Middle East!"

"In this final battle," C. C. Cribb, former president of Evangelical Ministries, Inc., wrote in 1977, "King Jesus will utterly devastate the assembled military millions of the diabolical dictator Antichrist."

Best-selling author Hal Lindsey interprets all of history—the Middle East and all the world—by his reading of Scripture. In *The Late Great Planet Earth*, he says the state of Israel is the dateline for all present and future major events.

"Before the Jews were a nation, nothing was relevant," Lindsey says. "Now when that occurred, there began to be a countdown of all kinds of prophetic signs falling into place. Because there had to be certain spheres of political power that would emerge, and

28

now, according to the prophetic pattern, the whole world would be focused on the Middle East and particularly Israel in the last days. All of the nations would be troubled and become involved with what goes on there. We can see how that's developing at this time, fitting right into the prophetic pattern by things as contemporary as things you see in the newspaper every day."

A former riverboat captain, who was born again and became a seminary student, Lindsey wrote four sequels to *The Late Great Planet Earth*, all involving biblical prophecy in which Israel plays a pivotal role.

As a purveyor of prophecy, Lindsey, whom I met at a 1985 Prayer Breakfast for Israel, has a considerable advantage over most of his predecessors and even his rivals. He is not a traditional hellfire and damnation preacher. Low-key and scholarly looking, Lindsey is about 50, with a full head of dark hair and a mustache. He has mastered the technique of sounding expert in world events and universal history. He gives the appearance of being compassionate, caring and concerned. As a speaker on the lecture circuit and on college campuses, where he appeared for eight years as a staff member of the Campus Crusade for Christ, Lindsey was popular as a propagator of standard apocalyptic prediction.

In his approach to Revelation, Lindsey uses what he calls a "deductive manner," attempting to deduce what God was trying to say through John's limited technical knowledge and vocabulary. For example, in his vision or dream, John sees locusts with scorpion tails. Lindsey conjectures that these are Cobra helicopters with some kind of nerve gas spraying from their tails.

Lindsey states categorically that the generation born since 1948 will witness the Second Coming of Christ. But before that event, we must fight both a "Gog-Magog" war and the battle of Armageddon. The holocaust will start like this: all the Arabs plus a Russian confederacy will invade Israel.

"Think of it," he writes in *There's a New World Coming*, "at least 200 million soldiers from the Orient, with millions more from the forces of the West headed by the Antichrist of the Revived Roman Empire (Western Europe)!

"Messiah Jesus will first strike those who have ravaged His city Jerusalem. Then he will strike the armies amassed in the valley of

Megiddo, or Armageddon. No wonder blood will stand to the horses' bridles for a distance of 200 miles from Jerusalem! . . . This whole valley will be filled with war materials, animals, bodies of men, and blood!

"It seems incredible! The human mind cannot conceive of such inhumanity of man to man, yet God will allow man's nature to fully display itself in that day," writes Lindsey.

Reading Lindsey, I find none of Saint Augustine's mournful mood in the face of war, as expressed in *The City of God.* Lindsey seems less than sad when he proclaims that every city in the world will be destroyed in a final nuclear war: "Imagine, cities like London, Paris, Tokyo, New York, Los Angeles, Chicago—obliterated!"

The eastern force alone will wipe out one-third of the world's population. Jesus, Lindsey writes, will "lay waste" to the earth and scorch its inhabitants. When the "great war" reaches such a pitch that almost everyone has been killed, there comes the "greatest moment"—Jesus saves humankind from total extinction by preserving a faithful remnant. In this hour those Jews who have not been slaughtered will convert to Christianity.

Only 144,000 Jews will remain alive after the battle of Armageddon, Lindsey says. And they all—every man, woman and child—will bow down to Jesus. As converted Christians, all the adults will at once begin preaching the gospel of Christ. "Imagine!" exults Lindsey. "They will be like 144,000 Jewish Billy Grahams turned loose at once!"

Jerry Falwell prefers the topic of Armageddon to almost any other subject. In a December 2, 1984, sermon, he began by reading Revelation 16:16—which gives us the first and only biblical mention of Armageddon, and then proclaimed:

"The word strikes fear into the hearts of people! There will be one last skirmish and then God will dispose of this Cosmos. The Scripture tells us in Revelation, chapters 21 and 22, God will destroy this earth—the heavens and the earth.

"And Peter says in his writings that the destruction will mount as with a fervent heat or a mighty explosion."

In the "holocaust at Armageddon," Falwell continues, "the Antichrist will move into the Middle East and place a statue of himself in the Jewish temple, the holy of holies, and demand that the whole world worship him as God . . .

"Millions of devout Jews will again be slaughtered at this time (Zechariah 15:8) but a remnant will escape (Zechariah 13:9) and God will supernaturally hide them for Himself for the last three and a half years of the Tribulation, some feel in the rose-red city of Petra (located in Jordan). I don't know how, but God will keep them because the Jews are the Chosen People of God."

The battlefield for Armageddon, says Falwell, quoting Zechariah 12:11 and Revelation 16:16, as well as Isaiah 34:35-36 and 36:1 "will stretch from Megiddo in the north to Edom on the south, a distance of about 200 miles. It will reach from the Mediterranean Sea on the west to the hills of Moab on the east, a distance of almost 100 miles. It will include the valley of Jehoshaphat—read Joel 3:2 and verse 12 as well. And the plains of Jezreel and the center of the entire area will be the city of Jerusalem—according to Zechariah 14, verses one and two.

"Into this area the multiplied millions of men at Armageddon—they will doubtless be approaching 400 million in number—will crowd in for that final holocaust of humanity and Joel 3:14 says the kings with their armies will come from the north and the south and the east and the west. In the most dramatic sense this will be the valley of decision for humanity, with a great wine press into which will be poured the fierceness of the wrath of Almighty God referred to in Revelation 19:15.

"Why will they be fighting there? Why is the Antichrist leading the armies of the world against Lord Jesus?

"Number one, because he hates the sovereignty of God. The battle has always been Satan versus Christ. That's the issue. Secondly, because of the deception of Satan, these nations will come. Third, because of the hatred of the nations for the Lord Jesus Christ. Some things will happen during that battle. The Euphrates river will dry up (Revelation 16:12) and the destruction of Jerusalem will occur."

Meanwhile, continues Falwell, quoting John's Revelation again, "all the fowls that fly in the heaven" will be feasting themselves on "the flesh of kings, the flesh of captains, the flesh of mighty men, the flesh of horses and their riders, and the flesh of all men, both free and slave, both small and great.

"John saw a beast in his dreams," Falwell concludes, and the kings of the earth with their armies gathered to make war against the Lord Jesus Christ, who, in John's vision, is a man sitting on a white horse.

As Armageddon draws to a close, with millions lying dead, the Lord Jesus will throw the beast and the false prophet (the Antichrist) "into the lake of fire that burns with brimstone." And the Lord Jesus will slay all His other enemies who somehow survived Armageddon.

Falwell had portrayed a horrifying picture of the end of the world. But he did not seem to be sad or even concerned. In fact he concluded this sermon by giving us a big smile and saying:

"Hey, it's great being a Christian! We have a wonderful future ahead!"

After listening to that sermon, I played tapes of "Dr. Jerry Falwell teaches Bible Prophecy" issued by the Old Time Gospel Hour in 1979. On these tapes Falwell says:

"So you see, Armageddon is a reality, a horrible reality. But, thank God, it's the end of the days of the Gentiles, for it then sets the stage for the introduction of the King, the Lord Jesus, in power and in great glory."

"Almost all Bible teachers I know are anticipating the Lord's imminent return. And I do believe myself that we are a part of that terminal generation, that last generation, that shall not pass until our Lord comes."

"There are some very recent developments in Russia, predicted by the prophet Ezekiel, which point up the soon return of our Lord. These communists are God-haters, they're Christ-rejecters, and their ultimate goal is world conquest. Some 26 hundred years ago, the Hebrew prophet Ezekiel prophesied that such a nation would rise to the north of Palestine just prior to the Second Coming of Christ.

"In Ezekiel, chapters 38 and 39, we read that the name of this land would be Rosh—that's Ezekiel 38, verse 2 in the American Standard Version—Rosh, R-O-S-H. He (Ezekiel) continues by mentioning two cities of Rosh. These he called Meshech and Tubal. That's all in verse 2, as well. The names here are remarkably similar to Moscow and Tubolsk, the two ruling capitals of Russia today.

Also, Ezekiel wrote that the land would be anti-God—verse 3—and therefore God would be against it. He also said that Russia or Rosh would invade Israel in the latter days—that's verse 8—then he said this invasion would be aided by various allies of Rosh—verses 5 and 6.

"He named those allies: Iran (which we have in the past called Persia), South Africa or Ethiopia, North Africa or Libya, Eastern Europe (called Gomer here in Ezekiel 38), and the Cossacks of southern Russia, called Togarmah in this chapter. In 38:15 of Ezekiel, the prophet describes the major part of horses in this invasion.

"The Cossacks of course have always owned and bred the largest and finest herd of horses in history. The purpose of this invasion, Ezekiel said, was to take a 'spoil'—verse 12, chapter 38. If one but removes the first two letters from this word 'spoil,' he soon realizes what Russia will really be after—obviously, oil. And that is where we find ourselves today. This, then, is Ezekiel's prophecy concerning Russia."

"In spite of the rosy and utterly unrealistic expectations by our government" (on the Camp David accords involving Israel and Egypt), "this treaty will not be a lasting treaty. We are certainly praying for the peace of Jerusalem. We certainly have the highest respect for the Prime Minister of Israel and the President of Egypt—great men, no doubt about that. And they certainly want peace—I am convinced that is true. But you and I know that there's not going to be any real peace in the Middle East until one day the Lord Jesus sits down upon the throne of David in Jerusalem."

"That day is coming. And for sure, you and I are going to be a part of it. But until then, there is not going to be any peace on this earth until the Prince of Peace, our Savior, returns."

Armageddon was much on Falwell's mind when he gave an interview, published March 4, 1981, in the *Los Angeles Times*, to reporter Robert Scheer. Their conversation went like this:

Scheer: "Turning to the future—in your pamphlet on Armageddon, you prophesy nuclear war with Russia."

Falwell: "We believe that Russia, because of her need of oil—and she's running out now—is going to move in on the Middle East, and particularly Israel because of their hatred of the Jew, and that it is at that time when all hell will break out. And it is at that time when I believe there will be some nuclear holocaust on this earth, because it says that blood shall flow in the streets up to the bridle of the horses in the Valley of Esdraelon for some 200 miles. And it speaks of horrible happenings that one can only relate in Second Peter 3, the melting of the elements, to nuclear warfare. But I think, at the end of the church age, when the church is Raptured, as we use the word, or cached out, then uninhibited hostilities will occur on this earth."

Scheer: "And Russia will be—"

Falwell: "And Russia will be the offender and will be ultimately totally destroyed."

Scheer: "Well, the whole world will, won't it?"

Falwell: "No, not the whole world, because then our Lord is coming back to the earth. First, He comes to take the church out. Seven years later, after Armageddon, this horrible holocaust, He's coming back to this very earth so it won't be destroyed, and the church is coming with him, to rule and reign with Christ on the earth for a thousand years. And then comes the new heavens and the new earth and eternity. That's all in that book on Armageddon—that is just an outline."

Scheer: "But will it be possible for Russia to be destroyed with nuclear weapons without it destroying the world?"

Falwell: "Yes, I don't mean that every person—Russia has many wonderful Christians there, too. The underground church is working very effectively in Russia, Red China. They're going to be taken out in the Rapture . . . It (the war) will come down out of the north—that has to be the Soviet Union—upon the midst of the earth—Israel and the Middle East—and so we believe the hostilities will be initiated by the Soviet Union. That's why most of us believe in the imminent return of Jesus Christ. We believe we're living in those days just prior to the Lord's coming."

Scheer: "By imminent, you mean a year or how long?"

Falwell: "Nobody is willing, of course—we're warned by the Lord not to set dates. The Lord said, 'No man knows the day or the hour.' Every religious group or leader who has ever set dates, I think, has dishonored the Lord and embarrassed themselves. It could be 50 years. I don't think so. I don't think we have that long.

I think we're coming to an impasse. All of history is reaching a climax and I do not think, I do not think we have 50 years left. I don't think my children will live their full lives out . . ."

In a tract, "Nuclear War and the Second Coming of Jesus Christ," published in 1983 by the Old-Time Gospel Hour, Falwell writes: "The Tribulation will result in such bloodshed and destruction that any war up to that time will seem insignificant."

In a chapter entitled "The Coming War with Russia," Falwell predicts a Soviet invasion of Israel followed by the annihilation of Soviet forces "on the mountains of Israel."

"At the conclusion of this battle, Scripture tells us that five-sixths (83 percent) of the Russian soldiers will have been destroyed (Ezekiel 39:2). The first grisly feast of God begins (Ezekiel 39:4,17-20). A similar feast would seem to take place later, after the battle of Armageddon (Revelation 19:17-18; Matthew 24:28). The communist threat will cease forever. Seven months will be spent in burying the dead (Ezekiel 39:11-15)."

The Saved
Will be Raptured

On the 1983 Falwell-sponsored tour, I remark to Clyde, who apparently has memorized much of the Old and New Testaments, that I am puzzled about how the Rapture will transpire. What does the Bible tell us about it?

"The term Rapture itself is not found in Scripture," Clyde said. "But it means 'the catching up.' It refers to the scene described in First Thessalonians 4:16-17: 'For the Lord Himself shall descend from heaven with a shout, with the voice of the archangel, and with the trumpet of God. And the dead in Christ shall rise first; then we who are alive and remain shall be caught up together with them in the clouds to meet the Lord in the air.' "

So, I ask Clyde, will Christ come to get the saved at the time of the Rapture?

"That is right."

And does He return a second time, or—considering His visit 2,000 years ago, it would now be the third time—to fight against the Antichrist in the battle of Armageddon?

"Yes," said Clyde. "That is right."

Since Clyde seems certain of this, I suggest that prophecy might fall into the category of "prewritten history."

"You must understand," Clyde explains, "that prophecy was a closed book until recently because God had instructed Daniel to seal the book 'until the time of the end.' That you find in Daniel 12:4."

Does Clyde believe that there are prophets today who are getting direct revelations from God?

"Not necessarily," Clyde said. "But we have men like Hal Lindsey and Jerry Falwell who have been given special insight into the prophetic word."

I recall to Clyde that once, as a child, returning home from school and not finding my mother, I feared she might have been Raptured—and thus lost forever to me on this earth.

"It can happen anytime," Clyde says. "I believe it is the next event. And millions will be caught up. Now in Florida I play golf with a neighbor who has not confessed Jesus Christ as his savior. I witness to him—that Christ can save him from damnation. And I warn him we are approaching the End of Time. We read in First ˈ ʰn, 'Children, it is the last hour; and as you have heard that Anti- cᴜ t is coming, so now many Antichrists have come; therefore we ᴎᴇᴡ that this is the last hour.'

And then of course we have the words of Jesus himself, in Revelation 22:20, 'Yes, I am coming soon.' "

And just how did Clyde expect the Rapture to work? How, I ask, will Christ pick and choose?

Clyde stares as if looking at a scene in the future. "I'm driving with my friend who is not saved, and the Rapture occurs, which, again, I expect any day, and I'm lifted up in the air out of the car. The car runs amok. And my friend is killed in the crash." Clyde then adds a sentence he likes to repeat, "I rejoice in the idea of meeting my Savior."

And what about his friend, with whom he played golf? Once Clyde is Raptured, safely awaiting the battle to end, will he be concerned about him?

"No, I need not be," he said. "The agony of friends and loved ones in hell will be entirely deleted from the mind of the survivors in heaven."

Clyde earlier told me his wife had died two years ago. Had she, I ask—and the others in his family—been saved?

"No, and that bothers me. Neither my wife, before she died, nor my son and his children—none of them are saved. They refused to confess Christ. I will be in heaven and I hate to say it, but I will not see them there. And I well know what is in store for those who have not bowed down before our Lord. We know from Zechariah 14:12 that the flesh of the wicked shall, on the last day, 'rot while they are still on their feet.' "

Clyde speaks of God's vengeance in a quiet voice. He seems certain his God will mete out to most of the dead and the currently alive—all who have not been born again—a punishment that denies any peace of annihilation.

In the everyday world, Clyde is soft-spoken, genial and considerate. He has been highly successful in his business. But his commitment is to another world, the world of his Rapture and his salvation. To him, this is reality, not just a world of apocalyptic visions. Emotionally he exists in his apocalyptic world, for it is more fascinating, providing him energy, sustenance and a tomorrow.

I can't help wondering: had Clyde forgotten that just as one may find a God of vengeance and hate in the Bible, one may also find a God of love and compassion? In his messages, Jesus calls us to be disarmed, to surrender, to be as little children, to forgive not seven times, but seven times seven.

We move on to discuss another perplexing question, never clear to me, even though I have heard several sermons on the subject of the Rapture. Just how long will born again Christians be up in heaven with Jesus?

"We will return to earth when Christ does—at the time of the great World War," Clyde says. "When He returns, He puts to death all the wicked. And the righteous who are left, the surviving Jews and Gentiles, are ushered into his thousand-year millennial reign, when Christ rules on earth as King of Kings for a thousand years. And we will be here with him.

"At the end of that thousand years, our present earth and heaven are destroyed and the new earth and new heaven are created, and in the new earth will be the new Jerusalem, the heavenly city, where the saved of all ages will live. And that begins eternity, and after that there are no more sequences of events. So the Rapture of the church is the first event in this whole series, and that can occur anytime."

I have been in remote corners of the world, I tell Clyde, where native peoples have not heard of Jesus Christ. Because of this, do they deserve to be assigned to an endless hell?

"We are now with short-wave radios, getting the message of Christ to all the areas of the world," Clyde said. "So many may still have time to repent of their sins and to accept Jesus Christ as their Savior."

Clyde and I then discuss the difference—as regards a Messiah—

between Judaism and Christianity.

"There's the story of a Jew and a Christian discussing this," Clyde relates. "They are both sitting and talking—and waiting. And they agree that the big question in each of their minds is, Has He been here before?

"I say we have a common destiny: the Jews today look for the Messiah to come. We Christians look for the Messiah to return. So when He does come, Christianity and Judaism will be united again because we will all recognize this is the Messiah we have been looking for."

Few if any rabbis or religious Jews, however, would say or feel this. Those who revere Judaism would resent Clyde's including all Jews as an abstract entity in his belief system, rendering them mere pawns and ultimately unimportant in his scheme of heaven and hell and his own salvation.

Clyde has a simple formula to deal with life's complexities such as atomic fallout, the pollution of our environment, the population explosion, widespread hunger, world deficit, higher taxes, less security.

For Clyde, Falwell, Lindsey and millions of others, the answer lies in one solution: "Get Right" with Jesus, and God's spirit will take up residence within you. And then, before the impending destruction of the world occurs, you as one of the saved will be taken from the earth. In Clyde's view one need not work to eliminate pollution in our cities or starvation in India and Africa. One need not concern oneself with nuclear proliferation. One need not attempt to prevent an Arab-Israeli war. Rather—pray for it to explode and engulf the world, since this is part of the divine scheme.

I heard Falwell sum up his reason why a nuclear Armageddon would not bother him. "You know why I'm not worried?" he said. "I ain't gonna be here."

Reagan: Arming
for a Real Armageddon

Did Ronald Reagan grow up with the same belief system as Clyde, Jerry Falwell, Jimmy Swaggart and other dispensationalists? Andrew Lang of Washington, D.C., who has made an in-depth study of Reagan and Armageddon theology, believes that he did.

"If Reagan was not a dispensationalist in the years of his presidency, he was earlier on. Remarks made by Reagan in the 1970s, and revealed for the first time in 1985, prove that Reagan was a dispensationalist—a believer in the ideology of Armageddon," said Lang, research director of the Christic Institute, a nonpartisan research center of Christians, Jews and Muslims. In 1984 the institute held a press conference on the subject of Reagan and Armageddon that produced headline stories in leading newspapers across the nation.

At that press conference, Lang said that he and others at the Christic Institute wanted to investigate Reagan and the subject of Armageddon theology "since the possibility that a president might personally believe God had foreordained a nuclear war raises a number of chilling questions: Would a dispensationalist president really believe in the feasibility of arms negotiations? In a nuclear crisis, would he be deliberate and rational? Or would he prove to be eager to push a button, and thereby, in his mind, perhaps, feel he was helping God in biblical, foreordained plans for the End of Time?"

Lang, who was aided in his study of Reagan and Armageddon by New York research-writer Larry Jones, a graduate of Columbia University, explained that "a dispensationalist, or believer in the ideology of Armageddon, is a fundamentalist who reads the Bible as an almanac to predict the future. Dispensationalists such as Jerry

Falwell, Hal Lindsey, Pat Robertson and other leaders of the New Christian Right believe that the Bible predicts the imminent Second Coming of Jesus Christ after a period of global nuclear warfare, natural disasters, economic collapse and social chaos.

"They believe these events have to happen before the Second Coming and they believe they are clearly outlined in the Bible. Before the last seven years of history, born again Christians will be physically lifted from the face of the earth and reunited with Christ in the air. From that vantage point they will safely watch the nuclear wars and economic crisis of the tribulation. At the end of the tribulation these born again Christians will return with Jesus Christ as their military commander to fight the battle of Armageddon, destroy God's enemies and then rule the earth for 1,000 years."

Did Reagan believe this?

Three sources shed light on the subject. First, his childhood, and the strong influence of a Bible-believing mother, Nelle Reagan. She "believed in the divine will perhaps to the point of predestination," writes Christian Broadcasting Network executive Bob Slosser in a Reagan biography, *Reagan Inside Out.* (Word Books, 1984).

"Ronald Reagan's mother, Nelle, was very influential on him in just about every way, particularly influential in young Reagan's spiritual upbringing," Slosser explained on a broadcast, "Ronald Reagan and the Prophecy of Armageddon," produced by New York WBAI radio reporter Joe Cuomo and heard on public radio stations in the fall of 1984.

"She—the Disciples of Christ was her denomination—faithfully attended services. She was a very devout woman, a Bible reader, thoroughly committed to Jesus Christ as Lord and Savior, and so as a result of that, Reagan was exposed to churchgoing and he was exposed to Bible reading and sort of just a natural outworking of what you might call a Christian life."

At times Reagan was embarrassed by his "extreme piety," Slosser said on the Cuomo show. Reagan worked out this piety, Slosser said, in "a manly, sort of Gary Cooper, Western kind of way." Instead of saying "The Lord made it plain to me," Reagan would say, "My first counselor told me." Those who knew Reagan knew he meant "the Lord." said Slosser, who concluded, "So you know, he has been greatly influenced down through the years by the teaching that he received from his mother in his early life."

Reagan admitted the tremendous influence of his early indoctrination. "You know I was raised on the Bible. I also taught it for
a long time in Sunday School," Reagan told writer William Rose
in a May, 1968 *Christian Life* article. Reagan taught Sunday School
at the First Christian Church in Dixon, Illinois while he was in high
school.

Reagan referred to his early indoctrination again in a 1980 interview. "I was fortunate," he told TV evangelist Jim Bakker. "I
had a mother who planted a great faith in me, much more than
I realized at the time she was doing it."

In addition to his Bible-believing mother, Reagan was influenced
by close friends, many of them dispensationalists who believe God
will both show special favors to and punish His Chosen People.

In the 1968 *Christian Life* article Reagan said that during a brief
stay in a hospital that year he had been visited by his Bel Air pastor
Donn Moomaw, a former all-American football player, and
Evangelist Billy Graham. Reagan then related this story:

"We got into a conversation about how many of the prophecies
concerning the Second Coming seemed to be having their fulfillment at this particular time. Graham told me how world leaders
who are students of the Bible and others who have studied it have
come to this same conclusion—that apparently never in history
have so many of the prophecies come true in such a relatively short
time. After the conversation I asked Donn to send me some more
material on prophecy so I could check them out in the Bible for
myself."

As governor of one of America's largest states, in territory and
population, Reagan was a busy chief executive. Yet, he took time
from his job as governor to study prophecy and the End of Time.
Apparently his own research into the Bible led him to accept, to
some extent at least, the doctrine that God had foreordained
millions of us living today would be killed in a final battle called
Armageddon.

On September 20, 1970, during Reagan's second campaign for
governor, Hollywood singer Pat Boone and his wife Shirley, and
two influential evangelical-charismatic Christians, George Otis and
Harald Bredesen, visited Reagan at his home in Sacramento, and
had a long talk about prophecy and the signs of the times, including

what Otis and Bredesen described as the "outpouring of the Holy Spirit." (Otis describes the meeting, which he terms a "Visit with a King," in his book, *High Adventure*. And Slosser reports on the same meeting in *Reagan Inside Out*).

At the end of their talk, both Otis and Slosser report, the men joined hands in prayer with Governor Reagan. Otis was overcome with the spirit and so, apparently, was Reagan. Otis prophesied Reagan's ascent to the presidency and Reagan's arms "shook and pulsated" while Otis prophesied.

On June 29, 1971 Governor Reagan asked Billy Graham to deliver a "spiritual State of the State" address to both houses of the California legislature. In his talk, Graham declared the only alternative to communism was "the plan in the Bible. The Bible says that man is going to go from trouble to trouble and judgment to judgment but there is going to come a day when God will intervene in the history of man and the Messiah is going to come."

Following the talk, Reagan honored Graham at a luncheon. Those attending included Reagan's cabinet and staff as well as the chairman of Graham's Sacramento crusades, realtor Walt Hanson.

During the meal, Hanson recalled to New York WBAI radio reporter Joe Cuomo, Graham and Reagan began talking about the Second Coming of the Lord Jesus Christ. And Reagan asked Graham, "Well, do you believe that Jesus Christ is coming soon, and what are the signs of His coming if that is the case?"

"The indication is . . . that Jesus Christ is at the very door," Graham told Reagan. "Christ could come at any time."

"Governor Reagan was very much at that point impressed and went along with it," Hanson reported on the Cuomo broadcast.

That same year—1971—Reagan read many popular books on the subject of Armageddon, among them Lindsey's *The Late Great Planet Earth*, which was "repeatedly discussed" that year, according to the governor's legal secretary, Herb Ellingwood speaking on the Cuomo radio program, "Ronald Reagan and the Prophecy of Armageddon." Ellingwood, one of the most fervent believers in the cult of Israel, including the necessity for a final battle, said he and Governor Reagan often sat together and discussed biblical prophecy. Reagan "quoted the Bible or referred to the Bible in a variety of ways," said Ellingwood who conducted daily prayer services with staff members praying exclusively for Reagan, while Reagan was governor.

Reagan often talked about prophecy. There was evidence in 1971 to indicate that Reagan, at least in that year, was a dispensationalist or a believer in the cult of Israel and the ideology of Armageddon. James Mills, formerly president pro tem of the California State Senate, in an August, 1985 *San Diego Magazine*, reports this incident:

It was the first year of then Governor Reagan's second term and Mills's first year as elected head of the State Senate. The two were sitting side by side at a lobbyists' banquet in Sacramento honoring Mills. Reagan, "with marvelous skill and infectious enjoyment," had related an amusing anecdote about Barney Old-field, the racecar driver. Reagan's mood changed abruptly, however, when the headwaiter dimmed the lights to prepare guests for the fiery entrance of cherries jubilee. As a waiter set two flaming bowls of cherries in front of Governor Reagan and Mills, Reagan turned to Mills and "totally unexpectedly" asked if he had ever read chapters 38 and 39 of Ezekiel.

Mills assured the governor that, having grown up in a house-hold of Bible-believing Baptists, he had read and discussed the Ezekiel passages that speak of Gog and Magog (which dispensationalists say mean Russia) many times, as well as other references to the End Times in the 16th and 19th chapters of the book of Revelation.

It was the "fierce Old Testament prophet of Ezekiel," Reagan said, who had best "foreseen the carnage that would destroy our age." At that point Reagan spoke with "firelit intensity" about Libya having gone communist. And insisted "that's a sign that the day of Armageddon isn't far off."

Mills then reminded Reagan that Ezekiel also says that Ethiopia will be among the evil powers. And Mills added, "I can't see Haile Selassie, the Lion of Judah, teaming up with a bunch of commies to make war on God's Chosen People."

"No," Reagan said. "I agree that everything hasn't fallen into place yet. But there is only that one thing left that has to happen. The Reds have to take over Ethiopia."

Mills said he did not think that very probable.

"I do, I think it's inevitable," Reagan insisted. "It's necessary to fulfill the prophecy that Ethiopia will be one of the ungodly nations that go against Israel." (Three years after their conversation, Mills noted in his article, the communists desposed Haile Selassie, and Reagan "may well have been gratified to see an apparent fulfillment of prophecy relating to the advent of the Messiah.")

At the 1971 dinner, Mills wrote, Reagan talked of a coming nuclear Armageddon "like a preacher to a skeptical college student." Reagan told Mills: "All of the other prophecies that had to be fulfilled before Armageddon have come to pass. In the 38th chapter of Ezekiel it says God will take the children of Israel from among the heathen, where they'd been scattered and will gather them again in the promised land. That has finally come about after 2,000 years. For the first time ever, everything is in place for the battle of Armageddon and the Second Coming of Christ."

When Mills reminded Reagan that "the one thing the Bible says most clearly about the Second Coming is that no one can know when it will happen," Reagan, his voice rising, more in pitch than in volume, replied:

"Everything is falling into place. It can't be too long now. Ezekiel says that fire and brimstone will be rained upon the enemies of God's people. That must mean that they'll be destroyed by nuclear weapons. They exist now, and they never did in the past.

"Ezekiel," Reagan continued, "tells us that Gog, the nation that will lead all of the other powers of darkness against Israel, will come out of the north. Biblical scholars have been saying for generations that Gog must be Russia. What other powerful nation is to the north of Israel? None. But it didn't seem to make sense before the Russian revolution, when Russia was a Christian country. Now it does, now that Russia has become communistic and atheistic, now that Russia has set itself against God. Now it fits the description of Gog perfectly."

Mills could not get Reagan's words out of his mind, and after the dinner he made copious notes of what Governor Reagan had said. Those notes, made in 1971, formed the basis for his 1985 article.

In 1976, Reagan discussed the Battle of Armageddon in a taped interview with a California associate, George Otis, mentioned previously as having prophesied Reagan's ascent to the presidency.

Otis, who in his book, *The Ghost of Hagar,* says he looks forward to the prophecied Gog/Magog war (interpreted as an invasion of Israel by the Soviets "in the near future"), asked if Reagan felt he would be Raptured and thereby escape the terrible period of Tribulation during the final battle—an escape made possible, in dispensationalist theology, only by being born again.

Was Reagan, Otis asked, born again?

"Yes," said Reagan. "I can't remember a time in my life when I didn't call upon God and hopefully thank Him as often as I called upon Him, and yet, yes, I have to believe within my own experience there came a time when there developed a new relationship and it grew out of need. And so yes," Reagan concluded, "I would say in the sense that I understand it, that I have had an experience that could be described as being born again."

Governor Reagan also talked about Armageddon to Evangelist Harald Bredesen of California. On one occasion, Bredesen, along with singer Pat Boone and George Otis, visited Reagan in his home. To Bredesen's "great pleasure and some little amazement" Governor Reagan impressed his visitors by ticking off biblical prophecies.

"First, that the Jew, if he was not faithful to God, would be scattered to the ends of the earth," Bredesen quoted Reagan as saying. "But that having happened, God would not wash His hands of them. Before the return of His Son, He would regather them to Israel and even the method of transportation they would be using would be detailed by the prophet. He said some would come by ship and others return as doves to their cotes. In other words, they'd come by ship or by plane. A nation would be born in a day . . .

"And of course he (Reagan) cited the fact that the promise that Jerusalem would be trodden under foot of the Gentiles until the time of the Gentiles was fulfilled. And this prophecy was fulfilled in 1967 when Jerusalem was reunited under the Israeli flag.

"What impressed me specially about it was the fact that I could see that Reagan had grown spiritually, tremendously," Bredesen continued. "A good example of his full awareness of what was going on, in terms of prophetic eschatology, was his ability to cite the very day in 1948 when Israel was reconstituted as a nation.

"I got the impression that Reagan was definitely aware of God's purposes for the Mideast," Bredesen concluded. "And for that reason felt the period which we're going through now is particularly significant, since the events projected in the Bible are coming to a head right at this time."

As a 1980 presidential candidate, Reagan continued to talk about Armageddon. "We may be the generation that sees Armageddon," Presidential candidate Reagan told evangelist Jim Bakker of the PTL network.

Evangelist author Doug Wead, present at that interview, reported he had often heard Reagan say the end of the world may be at hand. At a dinner party in the Reagans' California Pacific Palisades home, which the Weads attended, the conversation turned to the Soviet Union and Bible prophecy. In the midst of the discussion, Reagan, according to Wead, announced to his guests, "We could be the generation that sees Armageddon."

That was no chance remark. Reagan discussed Bible prophecy and eschatology as "common subjects," Wead said, adding that in interviews where he had been present, "I've heard him (Reagan) say, 'This could be the generation that sees Armageddon. This very well could be that generation.'"

In that same year, 1980, presidential candidate Reagan made yet another apocalyptic comment. As reported by *New York Times* columnist William Safire, Reagan was addressing a group of Jewish leaders when he said, "Israel is the only stable democracy we can rely on as a spot where Armageddon could come."

Reporter Robert Scheer in a March 1981 interview with Jerry Falwell revealed President Reagan had said the destruction of our world could indeed happen "very fast." "History is reaching a climax," Falwell told Scheer, adding he did not think we had 50 years left. Asked if Reagan agreed with him, Falwell said, "Yes, he does." Falwell added that Reagan had told him, "Jerry, I sometimes believe we're heading very fast for Armageddon right now."

Two years later, Reagan arranged for Falwell to attend National Security Council briefings and discuss with America's top officials plans for a nuclear war with Russia. Also, according to Hal Lindsey, Reagan also approved of *The Late Great Planet Earth* dispensationalist author giving a talk on a nuclear war with Russia to Pentagon strategists.

One October day in 1983, Reagan revealed that Armageddon continued to occupy his mind. He telephoned Tom Dine of the American Israel Public Affairs Committee, the most powerful of the pro-Israel lobbies. According to Dine, President Reagan said: "You know, I turn back to your ancient prophets in the Old Testament and the signs foretelling Armageddon, and I find myself wondering if we're the generation that's going to see that come about. I don't know if you've noted any of those prophecies lately, but believe me, they certainly describe the times we're going through."

On three occasions, in 1982, 1983 and 1984, Reagan addressed the National Religious Broadcasters (NRB), composed for the most part of dispensationalists who believe a nuclear war is approaching.

"Maybe it's later than we think," Reagan told cheering NRB members in 1982. An Armageddon, in their minds, will usher in the Second Coming of Christ.

In 1983, Reagan revealed the importance of the Bible in his life, telling the NRB, "Within the covers of that single book are all the answers to all the problems that face us today."

In 1984, addressing 4,000 NRB delegates, Reagan indicated that he agrees with those who say, "Better dead than red." To reveal his own feelings on the matter, Reagan told a story of once having sat on a podium at a Los Angeles religious gathering when singer Pat Boone was a featured speaker. Boone's two daughters were little girls then, and Boone said that while he loved them more than anything on earth, "I would rather that they die now believing in God than grow up under communism." Reagan, in his 1984 NRB talk, praised Boone for having come out so strongly against the evils of communism. Until Boone did so, Reagan said, "I had underestimated him."

Most ardent dispensationalists see Russia as satanic—the evil empire. On March 8, 1983, Reagan spelled this out. "They (the Soviet Union) are the focus of evil in the modern world." Speaking to the National Association of Evangelicals, he added, "I believe that communism is another sad, bizarre chapter in human history whose last pages even now are being written."

James Mills, in the forementioned *San Diego Magazine* article, says Reagan's use in 1983 of the phrase "evil empire" to describe the Soviet Union "was not just rhetoric calculated to appeal to religious and political fundamentalists." It was, rather, a declaration that arose "from the beliefs he had expressed to me that night in 1971."

As president, Reagan "consistently manifested a commitment to discharge his duties in accordance with God's will, as any true believer holding high office should try to do," Mills wrote in his article, adding that Reagan felt that obligation especially as he sought to build up the military might of the United States and its allies.

"It is true that Ezekiel prophesied the victory of the armies of Israel and her allies in their terrible battle against the powers of darkness. However, conservative Christians like our president are not allowed the spiritual luxury of taking that victory for granted. Making the forces of righteousness strong to win that all-important conflict is, in such men's eyes, acting in fulfillment of God's prophecies and in accordance with His divine will, to the end that Christ will come again to reign over the earth for a thousand years.

"If Reagan now believes what he said to me in 1971—and whether he does or doesn't has been the subject of much speculation by newspaper columnists in the last few years—I have no doubt that is how he sees his responsibilities as the leader of the Western world. And it appears to me that most of his policy decisions are influenced by that perception.

"Certainly his attitudes relative to military spending, and his coolness to all proposals for nuclear disarmament, are consistent with such apocalyptic views," Mills continued. "Armageddon, as foreseen in the books of Ezekiel and Revelation, cannot take place in a world that has been disarmed. Anyone who believes it will come to pass cannot expect that disaramament will ever come about. It is contrary to God's plan as set forth in His word.

"The President's domestic and monetary policies, too, are in harmony with a literal interpretation of biblical prophecies," Mills continued. "There is no reason to get wrought up about the national debt if God is soon going to foreclose on the whole world.

"His support of gung-ho neo-conservatives like James Watt makes sense if seen in that way, too. Why be concerned about conservation? Why waste time and money preserving things for future generations when everything is going to come to a fiery end with this one?"

As a policy goal, "the implementation of the return of Christ to the earth hardly admits of competition for funds by outfits like Amtrak. It follows that all domestic programs, especially those that entail capital outlay, can and should be curtailed to free up money to finance the development of nuclear weapons in order to rain fiery destruction upon the evil enemies of God and His people."

One of the most striking thoughts expressed by James Mills in his article, it seemed to me, was his statement that Armageddon "cannot take place in a world that has been disarmed."

Yet, every nation is building more arms—and none more rapidly than the United States. Today, according to *Nuclear Battlefields* by William M. Arkin and Richard W. Fieldhouse, the United States has 670 nuclear-weapons facilities in 40 states for a total of 14,599 warhead deployments. West Germany hosts 3,396 U.S. nuclear weapons; Britain 1,268; Italy 549; Turkey 489; Greece 164; South Korea 151; the Netherlands 81 and Belgium 25.

The total destruction power of nuclear force in the world today, former Secretary of Defense Clark Clifford on August 14, 1985, told the Washington, D.C., National Press Club, "is one million times the force of the bomb we dropped on Hiroshima." Yet, Clifford asked, what do we do? "We go right on making more."

Since George Bush became president, we have no indication that he personally endorses Armageddon theology. But reporters such as Elinor Brecher of the Louisville, Kentucky *Courier Journal* (September 25, 1988) and Liz Smith of the New York *Daily News* (October 3, 1988) have raised questions regarding the religious convictions of Dan and Marilyn Quayle. They have reported that the parents of both Dan and Marilyn Quayle are avid followers of Col. Robert B. Thieme, Jr. of Houston, a dispensationalist described as "far to the right of Jerry Falwell." I heard Marilyn Quayle on ABC-TV defend her religious beliefs and those of her husband. She said a person's religion was his or her own personal business. But because Dan Quayle is near "the button," his theology as regards Armageddon becomes more than his personal business. Whether he believes in a God who would want the destruction of planet Earth becomes "the business" of us all.

A Rest Stop in Nazareth

The Falwell-sponsored tour in 1983 was typical of most organized tours in that the quoted price was based on double occupancy
of rooms. A single person could get single accommodations by paying a supplemental fee. I opted for the minimum price, based on
a double occupancy. And the Moral Majority in Lynchburg chose
my roommate. On the first night, after the group checked into a
Tel Aviv hotel, I took my bag to an assigned room and shortly
thereafter my roommate, whom I had not previously met, appeared.
Her name, she said, was Mona.

She was about 55, somewhat short and sturdily built. Her husband, she explained, had wanted to come on the trip, but could
not leave his job with the postal service. Formerly, they had lived
in Indiana but were now living in Florida. Mona was dressed in
wash-and-wear nylon attire, and she wore a lapel pin pronouncing,
"Israel, we love you because God loves you." As I came to know
her better, I noticed that she always carried a Bible and often referred to it as a guide for everyday living. She was soft-spoken,
considerate—never overstaying in the bathroom—and all in all an
accommodating, pleasant roommate.

One day after visiting the Sea of Galilee, we boarded our bus
for a drive to Jerusalem. It was five o'clock and after we were seated,
our Israeli guide told us, "We've about a two-and-a-half-hour drive.
You won't see anything, so why don't you put your heads back,
close your eyes and take a siesta." The pilgrims reclined their heads
and closed their eyes. We were entering into the West Bank land
of the Palestinians, but our guide did not mention West Bank or
Palestinians.

Mona, I whispered to my roommate, who sat beside me, we are

51

passing through the land of the Palestinians. There are Palestinian homes and Palestinians all around us. They have always lived here.

I pointed to a small stream, the Jordan River, so famous in our Christian hymns, that flowed on our left. Mona, I continued, this land is inhabited by Palestinians, but our guide does not mention this. Rather, he calls this land by the old biblical names of Judea and Samaria. But for more than three million Palestinians, this is Palestine.

The West Bank together with a section called the Gaza Strip comprise about a quarter of former Palestine. These areas are inhabited by about 1.2 million Palestinians. More than 400,000 live in the Gaza Strip and 800,000 in the West Bank, including 105,000 residents of Arab East Jerusalem. These Palestinians form a third of the Palestinian people. Another half million Palestinians live inside Israel, and more than 1.5 million live in exile in Jordan, Lebanon, Syria, the United States and other countries.

The area of the West Bank through which we were passing was inhabited exclusively by Palestinians until the 1967 war. At the end of that war, which resulted in an Israeli victory, the Israelis began to build Jewish settlements on the Palestinian land. Their settlements have been condemned by every world leader and ruled illegal by all international courts. The building of the settlements has steadily increased, however, and many believe the West Bank is already well on its way to becoming part of the Zionist empire.

In 1983 Jews controlled about 40 percent of the land, which they had carved into a network of roads, waterways and electrical grids. In that year more than 25,000 Jewish settlers—about one-third of them from the United States—were living in illegal West Bank colonies.

Dusk was bringing mysterious colors to the land. We saw flickering lights of villages in the distance. As I whispered my comments about Palestinians being all around us, I could see Mona's body undergo a transformation. I saw her shoulders move forward in an encapsulating, protective, defensive stance, as if I were literally assaulting her with a weapon. She was attempting to avoid hearing what she had assumed she should not know. Eventually she asked:

"Palestinians? Who are Palestinians? Isn't *everyone* living here Jewish?"

That, of course, was the way she had read it in the parts of the Bible familiar to her. Mona read her Bible every day. But she knew little or nothing about current Middle East history or any of the events that had occurred since the Hebrews, for a short time, controlled Jerusalem. That one brief period, out of the dozens of conquests by various tribes, was the only history engraved on Mona's mind. It was as if, in studying English or European history, she had read about events before and during the time of Christ but failed to study, read, or talk about events that had transpired since then. Rather, she had her mind fixed on one time frame—and only one tribal people.

In our religious, fundamentalist backgrounds, Mona and I were very much alike. We both had grown up in Christian homes, listening to and reading the Bible. We had not learned about the Middle East in our schools but knew only what we had read in Scripture penned by the Hebrews. We both had studied the Old Testament stories of the Hebrew people's sojourn in Palestine, the wars of the kings of Israel and the special dealings of God with the Chosen People. Like millions of other Christian children, we read stories about Abraham, Moses, Joshua, David and Solomon, who we assumed were the principal heroes in all Middle East history. And, for that matter, the heroes of all peoples everywhere—including the Chinese, Indians, Egyptians, Persians, and Japanese.

Growing up, neither of us learned that the Hebrews were a tribal group like many other tribal groups before as well as later, who held control of Jerusalem only for a brief span of time.

Rather, we came not only to focus on the Hebrews as if they had discovered Palestine, but to believe that it was a land without any people until the Hebrews arrived. In our young minds the Hebrews were the earliest of people, coming along shortly after Adam and Eve. And when we did begin to read or hear about other Middle Eastern peoples, we did not accept them as real people, but only as the enemies of the Hebrew authors and automatically the enemies of God.

As children, Mona and I listened to stories of a covenant, which we and millions of other fundamentalists came to understand to be a special relationship that God made with his Chosen People. We were taught to believe those Old Testament authors who declared themselves and their tribe to be the favorite people of God. In my own childhood, I could never have imagined that this concept might one day lead to the uprooting of non-Jews and recurring wars.

After a silence, Mona, as if pleading for reassurance that non-Jews did not exist in this land, asked:

"Are the Palestinians also Jews?"

Palestinians, I reminded her, were Christians and Muslims.

"Well," she replied, closing her eyes, "It is all too complicated for me."

Mona wanted to sleep. And I did not disturb her further. I had failed to reach her mind. She had firmly accepted the Holy Land on emotional terms. And, as psychologists remind us, in a conflict between rational thought and deep feelings, we are swayed more easily and deeply by emotions.

Mona had learned from mentors such as Falwell that man-made laws do not apply to Israel. She had been taught that of all the peoples in the world, only the Israelis do not come under the laws of men, but rather the law of God.

If Mona had been led to believe that God favors Jews but not Palestinians, whether Christians or Muslims, then, as a Christian, she must make native Christians and Muslims invisible or treat them as one stereotypical whole, or dismiss them as mere pawns in a divine chess game. As in any form of racism, she blocked from view their political, religious, and cultural diversity. A Christian such as Mona who accepts the cult of a Chosen People will lose some of her capacity to understand, to feel compassion. And she will even lose the concept that Palestinian Christians and Muslims share human traits and a human existence with other Christians such as herself.

Mona was no different from most of the other Christians who were on our tour. They, too, having accepted the concept of a Chosen People, had also accepted a concept of an unChosen People. They placed the Chosen and the unChosen into their system of belief that calls for the Jews to be in Palestine—and the native Christians and Muslims who have for centuries lived in Palestine, to be outside (whether they were or not). If actually there, then they were the absent present and invisible.

On one occasion, however, we passed a site where Palestinians seemed entirely visible. It was a large refugee camp for Muslims and Christians who once lived on the land where Israelis now reside.

"What is this?" Elizabeth, a retired school teacher from New Jersey, called out.

"Arabs live there," our Israeli guide said. "They prefer to live like that."

"We tried to be friends with the Arabs," our guide continued, "but these Muslims are all terrorists." In his comment, he ignored the presence of the local Christian communities and represented all Palestinians as Muslims—enemies of God and His Chosen People. As the guide spoke, I watched Elizabeth, who sat in a seat directly in front of me, nod her head in agreement. I touched her on the shoulder, asking:

Was she, knowing that our guide and most other Israelis see the Arabs as enemies, viewing them as her enemies, also?

"If Arabs are enemies of Israel," said Elizabeth, "it follows they are enemies of God."

Clearly, Elizabeth was assuming that, by the act of having lived on the land for so long, the Palestinians stand in defiance of the Almighty. Elizabeth was not one of the Christians who fuel anti-Semitism against the Jews by calling them killers of Christ. Rather, she was one of the Christians who fuel a new anti-Semitism with a contempt for other Semites, the indigenous people of Palestine.

It seemed natural to me that we would be interested in meeting Palestinian Christians. Travelers often seek out familiar religious affiliates when traveling abroad. Delegations of American Jews, for instance, traveling to Moscow, want to meet Soviet Jews, and when they go to Jerusalem, they meet Israeli Jews. But Jerry Falwell and his group ignored—and deliberately chose not to see—the Christians who were all around us.

Palestinian Christians in Jerusalem own and operate restaurants—but we as Christians on the Falwell junket did not visit or eat in any one of these. Palestinian Christians own hotels in Jerusalem, but we did not stay in any. Christians also own and operate bus lines and travel agencies, but we did not meet any of them.

On the tour, I carried the names of a number of Christian organizations and Christian leaders now living in and near Jerusalem. From my previous stay in the Holy Land in 1979-1980, and from American Christian friends I had names and addresses of a number of Christians including the Reverend Audeh Rantisi, head of the Evangelical Home in Ramallah and acting mayor of that city; two American professors, Shirley and Hugh Harcourt—as well as a Christian journalist, Raymonda Tawil, and Henry Selz, representative for the American Near East Refugee Aid (ANERA) in Jerusalem.

I also carried names of Christians given me by Dr. Landrum Bolling, head of the Ecumenical Center at Tantur, near Bethlehem; the Reverend O. Kelly Ingram of Duke University Divinity School, and Professor David M. Graybeal of Drew University's Theological School.

Additionally, I had the names of Mr. and Mrs. Earl Morgan, as well as Marilyn Hunter, who were serving as lay leaders with the Church of the Nazarene in Nazareth. I asked our guide to please permit us the time to meet the American Nazarenes when our bus reached Nazareth.

Since the time of Christ, Nazareth, along with Bethlehem and Jerusalem, has been an important Christian town and remains so today. Nazareth was the town where Jesus lived and where he grew to manhood. It was in Nazareth that Jesus preached his first known sermon and was nearly killed when he spoke comparatively favorably about a Lebanese (Sidonian) widow and a Syrian soldier. (Luke 4:26-9).

However, our Israeli guide did not tell us much about towns inhabited predominantly by Palestinian Christians. Since the creation of the Jewish state, it has been Israeli policy not to recognize the existence of the Palestinians. Former Prime Minister Golda Meir summed up this policy when she stated: "There is no Palestinian people."

The evening before our group was scheduled to visit Nazareth, our Israeli guide announced to our group that we would not stop in Nazareth. He perhaps made the announcement to deal in advance with objections any of us might have to not visiting one of the three principal Christian towns. Since he obviously had decided not to comply with my request, I said nothing further. And no one else in the group questioned his decision or asked why we would not visit the town where Jesus, known as the man from Nazareth, spent all of his years from age 12 to 30.

As our bus approached the famous Christian town, we saw that it is situated in a basin in the south side of a hill. To the north, we saw a beautiful panorama of fertile valleys and hills, with snow-capped Mount Hermon in the distance. Looking to the south, we saw the Plain of Esdraelon that extends from the Jordan River to the Mediterranean. Ten miles to the west of Nazareth we saw Mount Carmel, where Elijah in his contest with the priests of Baal called down fire from heaven.

On the outskirts of Nazareth, our guide said, in reference to the announcement made by God to Mary that she would conceive and give birth to Jesus: "You could go to that church there,"—and he pointed to the Church of the Annunciation in the distance. "But there are 32 other churches that claim to be the site, so why go to any of them?" The Christians laughed about that and agreed to take no interest in Nazareth. However, our guide did change his mind about making a stop.

"We will stop in Nazareth for 20 minutes," he said, "to use toilet facilities."

And the bus did stop. Everyone went into a shop with toilet facilities. And within 20 minutes we reboarded the bus.

Then we left Nazareth without having seen it. I tried to imagine a Buddhist going to see the Kamakura Buddha in Tokyo or a Muslim going to Mecca, or a Jew making a journey to the Wailing Wall only "to use the toilet facilities."

Our leaders, it appeared to me, made a special effort to keep all of us isolated from Christians—native Palestinian Christians as well as Christians from other countries, including the United States, living in the Holy Land. On a Sunday, someone suggested: "Why don't we go to a church service?" The request was sent to Falwell, who—although there are several dozen Christian churches throughout Jerusalem—announced that we would have a "church" service in an Israeli hotel.

In stating that it seemed natural to me that Christians traveling from America would want to meet Christians living in the Holy

Land, I do not mean to imply that I am more interested in them than Muslims, Jews or atheists. However, since we were Christians on a tour of the Land of Christ, presumably to learn about Christ, one might assume that native Christians, whose forebears date back to Christ himself, could make a contribution on the subject of Christianity.

Yet because of Falwell's presumption that the Palestinians were not there, our group was encapsulated, as in a space ship, and unaware of the reality outside our air-conditioned bus. By not recognizing one party to the Palestinian-Israeli conflict, the Falwell-sponsored Christians ignored the reality of the war between the Palestinians and the state of Israel that raged around us.

The pilgrims missed learning about the religious implications of this war, and its political significance in all our lives, as well. I felt we could have been helped by meeting Christians who, for over a century, since the first stirrings of Arab nationalism, have been at the center of the internal politics of the Middle East.

Meeting with native Christians might have enabled us to understand more of the ferment of the Middle East, where most of the people are ruled by totalitarian regimes characterized by a one-party system.

We might have come to understand, in addition, why the peoples of the Middle East, including the Christians, are going through a new crisis of identity. And why they are challenging the idea of nationalism, with which they are attempting to identify. And why individuals and communities are now attempting to redefine their identities along ethnic and religious terms.

Had we met indigenous Christians, we might have asked, What does it means to be a Christian in the Middle East today? Is your faith in power, and therefore in powerful institutions? How do you relate to the Muslims and Jews? Do you relate only on the basis of a balance of power? Or do you as Christians see your power as the power of sacrifice?

Falwell, however, did not instruct his followers about real times in a real place where real people of three major religions struggle to coexist on grounds held sacred by all three. Rather, he presented the Holy Land as an Edenic fulfillment of God's promises to only one group of people. The rest, as Golda Meir had said, did not exist.

Applauding a
Military Messiah

In his sponsorship of tours to the Holy Land, Jerry Falwell does not himself go over with the group. Nor does he accompany the Christians to any Christian site, such as the Church of the Nativity in Bethlehem, the Mount of the Beatitudes, the Sea of Galilee, Nazareth or any of the holy Christian sites in Jerusalem. Rather, Falwell flies over first class, goes to a first class Jerusalem hotel, meets with top Israeli military and governmental figures and talks politics. In short, he stays in the Holy Land—and only in Jerusalem—for the last three days of the tour.

I will pinpoint the time and place when I first learned that Falwell himself would not accompany the group:

It is November 13, 1983, and I am seated alone at JFK airport, having checked in for the El Al flight designated by the sponsoring group, Falwell's Moral Majority.

Four women approach me, asking, was I with the Moral Majority? I nod a greeting, we exchange names and locate a coffee shop, where we become better acquainted. Virginia Bolton is traveling with her pretty, dark-haired daughter, Jerrie. Peggy Jinks, blond and in her mid-forties, is traveling with her stunningly attractive blond teen-age daughter, Jamie. The Boltons are from Bainbridge, Georgia, and Peggy and Jamie Jinks are from Colquitt, Georgia.

As we chat, Peggy volunteers that Jerry Falwell—she says she feels she knows him personally by regularly listening to him on TV—will not be traveling with us. He will not be on any of the three planes used by the 630 pilgrims, Peggy explains, "because he would not want to risk our security."

"Bless his heart!" intones Virginia. "This is the price one pays for being a leader!"

One evening after our leader's arrival in Jerusalem—it is Saturday night, November 19, 1983—all 630 of us gather in the Diplomat Hotel auditorium. We anticipate a big event: Falwell has promised he will introduce us to Defense Minister Moshe Arens, former Israeli ambassador to the United States.

Seated in the auditorium, I look out to twelve flags of Israel and twelve American flags that are placed symbiotically two by two. I note that Falwell, seated on the podium, appears excited and happy, his alert eyes focused on a door at the rear of the auditorium through which the main celebrity of the evening will pass. We continue to sing hymns as the anticipation for the star attraction builds. Soon we experience a hushed silence and hear the marching of feet. The defense minister, in a suit with open-neck shirt, appears with four armed bodyguards and walks toward the podium.

As they march past me, I have time to reflect that in few other countries of the world does one see more armed men than in Israel. The ratio of soldiers to civilians in a country of fewer than four million is one to 22—by far the highest in the world. How sad a development that Israel, proclaimed as a haven for the world's Jews, has become one of the least safe places for Jews to live. As they build more weapons, they grow more fearful, less secure. Ironically, the danger of total collapse and disintegration comes from within, rather than from the enemies with whom they have fought so many wars.

To enthusiastic applause, Falwell introduces the U.S.-born graduate of the Massachusetts Institute of Technology. Arens begins by boasting that Israel's military operation in Lebanon "achieved a great victory, not only for Israel, but for the free world. We went into Lebanon to kill all the terrorists. We wanted to wipe them out." As he talks of slaughtering enemies, I sense a transformation in the usually soft-spoken, well-mannered Christians. They are energized, the adrenalin is flowing, as if a lion has been loose in our midst.

Arens talks of an Israeli army going back into Lebanon and Syria, and the Christians jump to their feet in sustained applause. Waving an arm, perhaps in the direction of Syria and the Soviet Union, he speaks of "enemies" and "communists" and says, "If the United States will fight alongside us, we will finish the job!"

As Arens calls for renewed dedication to military strength and a new and bigger war, the Christians interrupt him 18 times with standing ovations. All around me, I see men and women applauding wildly, stamping their feet and shouting "Amen!" and "Hallelujah!"

Afterwards, as we are leaving the auditorium, I ask George, a Texan who sells satellite dishes, Did he realize our group was applauding an invasion and the slaughtering of innocent people?

"Oh," he replies, "the invasion of Lebanon was God's will. It was a sacred war. I thought the invasion of Lebanon was great. It was right out of the Old Testament and confirms biblical prophecy. You know, this could mean we are nearing Armageddon—" As he pauses, anticipating such a nuclear holocaust, I see his eyes widen and his face brighten.

On another day our group visited Caesarea Philippi, north of Jerusalem, an ancient Roman stronghold where Philip, the son of Herod the Great, built a Roman temple in which he placed statues of Augustus and Tiberius and issued coins with the Temple of Zeus on one side. But the site is famous for another reason. It was here that Jesus questioned his disciples, asking if they really knew Him— if they truly understood His mission. And it was here that Peter answered Jesus, saying, "Thou art the Messiah, the Christ."

The tour—and Falwell's obvious interpretation of Jesus Christ as a military conqueror—prompted me to rethink my own interpretation of Christ. And to ask myself how I would answer Christ if He asked, "Who do you say that I am?"

Leaving Caesarea Philippi, I strike up a conversation with a man of our group named Chester, in his 60s, who describes himself as a lay preacher. It is my understanding, I say to Chester, that Peter was referring to a military Messiah. And rather than praise Peter, Jesus rebuked him, saying "Get thee behind me, Satan." And that Christ rebuked Peter because He was not taking the role of military conqueror.

"Yes, that is absolutely right!" Chester replies. "In fact, the disciples never really learned that lesson. You recall that even after the Last Supper with Christ, Peter wanted to go out with his sword and use it against his enemies.

"And it wasn't until later that they realized that He was the suffering servant of Isaiah," Chester continued. "And when the disciples started going back over the life of Jesus, they could see all the signs He had given them—revealing that He was taking a non-military role. And in fact, he had tried to teach them a principle: those who live by the sword die by the sword."

It all is so confusing, I tell Chester. Because it seems to me that Israel is going down the path of militarism, with huge defense budgets. And Falwell invites a military man to address us. Arens was, in fact, the star attraction offered to us Christians. And we applauded. So it seems to be a military Messiah we are applauding.

"Well," Chester said, "that's true."

I am now more perplexed than ever. If we Christians are supposed to follow Christ as the suffering servant, why should we be applauding a military Messiah?

Chester pauses for a moment and then quotes me the words of Jerry Falwell: "Because in the Bible it says that those who bless Israel, God will bless. And those who curse Israel will be accursed by God."

That's where I get really confused, I admit. If God wants people to follow the role of His son, the non-militaristic Messiah, and if Israel, by being highly militarized is sinning, I do not understand why God would bless the United States and Christians in the United States who are aiding and abetting the sinner.

Chester pauses. "Well, it doesn't make much sense," he admits. "But that's the way it is!"

My persistence in raising the issue of our group not having had the opportunity of meeting a single Christian—Palestinian Christian or any Christian from any land, serving in Nazareth, Jerusalem or Bethlehem—may have influenced Brother Greg Dixon, who served as aide to Falwell on this tour, to persuade Falwell to produce for the group at least one token native Christian. This is the scene:

We are in a large hotel auditorium. Falwell is speaking, and soon he is introducing a Baptist, a native of the Holy Land. Falwell does not, however, present the Baptist, who is sitting on the podium with Cal Thomas of the Moral Majority, as a Christian or a Palestinian. Rather, he presents the token Palestinian Christian simply as a "a man of God."

"This man is doing what I believe in doing, he is preaching the gospel to his own people," Falwell intones. "I kinda' have an affinity with him. I am pastor of a church in Lynchburg, Virginia, where I was born and raised." Turning to the guest, whose name is Naim Khoury, Falwell asks:

"Naim, where were you born?"

"Jerusalem."

"How many miles from Bethlehem?"

"Five miles."

"And I am preaching about five miles from where I was born in Virginia," Falwell says. And then he tells our group: "I want to do something for this man tonight. We are not going to have a cash offering tonight or tomorrow night. This is the only one, right here, now. I know some of you birds are loaded. (Laughter) I am a Baptist, I know how the Lord has blessed you—and so forth. Now I want tonight to invest in what God is doing with this man, right here. I don't give to programs, I give to men of God.

"Now I happen to have a 100-dollar bill in my pocket. I'm going to tell you whose picture is on it, in just a moment . . . [pause] . . . Jack Wyrtzen's." (This draws more laughter—Wyrtzen being a popular evangelical personality, traveling with our group). Falwell turns to an assistant on the podium, asking, "Whose name is that? I can't see it."

"Benjamin Franklin's."

"I want (aside to photographer) to have a picture taken of me giving $100. Now I want you to take a picture of everybody else, while they do the same thing." (Laughter) "I want everybody to write a check. Now you say, 'If I write a check, how do I make it out?' First Bible Baptist Church of Bethlehem. Just start writing! My goodness, get moving! And if you don't want to write a check, give ten dollars, give one hundred, five hundred—everybody give something. And make your check to the First Bible Baptist Church of Bethlehem."

Someone comes forward with a package of money. Falwell asks, "What is it? Israeli money? Now listen carefully, does everybody have your money out?" Cardboard boxes are passed and most everyone puts in money. Then, Dr. Naim Khoury speaks to us:

"I was born again 15 years ago in Jerusalem. I went to the States to get my education in the Baptist Bible College in Springfield,

Missouri, and four years ago came back to start the First Bible Baptist Church of Bethlehem. We had two people that first day and now we are running around 200. We have seen 500 people come to know the Lord Jesus Christ in this four-year period. It is known Jesus Christ was born 2,000 years ago and I am glad there is room for Jesus in the hearts of people in Bethlehem today."

Then Dr. Khoury sits down. I record his entire message, which is noteworthy for its brevity. After the meeting that night, I find Naim Khoury standing alone, and I ask if his converts are all Arabs.

"Yes," he says. "They are."

And do the Israelis permit him to speak to Jews about Christ?

"No, that is not permitted."

What about the suffering of Palestinian Christians and Muslims living under Israeli domination? Does he see this suffering?

"Yes."

But why, I persist, does he not speak out against this oppression? He remains silent.

I wonder how much money Falwell collected for him that evening. Guessing, I ask: Was it $5,000?

"Seven thousand," he replies.

This one Palestinian, among 100,000 Christians living in Israel and the occupied territories, was the only one we were officially permitted to see and hear. He told us little.

"I would have been most happy to have welcomed Falwell's group to Bethlehem," the mayor of Bethlehem and a well-known Christian, Elias Freij, told me. Freij, whose forebears have been Christians for nearly 2,000 years, said 14 million Christians live in the Middle East.

One day just prior to leaving Jerusalem, I sought out on my own Brother Joseph Loewenstein, a Christian and President Emeritus of Bethlehem University, with offices within the old walled city. As we sat over small cups of Arabic coffee, I asked him how the Israelis benefited by encouraging Falwell's followers to negate—to make invisible—the native Christians.

"The main goal of militant Zionists is to control the hearts and minds of the American Christians," he began. "If they can convince American Christians that the Palestinian people do not exist, or that they do not matter, then whatever the Israelis do, the Christians will approve.

"The Israeli stranglehold over Palestine means that the older Christians will stay—and die—and the younger Christians who cannot leave will have to remain, but they will not find a future here. The Zionists continue their illegal settlements on Palestinian land. The Palestinians continually lose land, and nobody seems to do anything about it. I am not at all pleased with the American policy, which goes along with the Israeli takeover. I consider it the genocide of the Palestinian people—without the furnaces.

"The Christians who are leaving or dying under this oppressive yoke are the same Christians who throughout Christian history have continually kept alive the flame of the mother church. Now they are enduring their greatest persecution since Christ called them to forsake all that Falwell now espouses—power and a 'king' such as Begin, Arens or Sharon. If Christ had been Falwell, he would have approved everything that was wrong, and would not have died on a cross.

"Falwell comes to Jerusalem. There are Christians all around him, but he refuses to see them. He closes his eyes and his heart to Christians who have lived here since the time of Christ. He forsakes the suffering—to please the Zionists. Falwell would have the Christians revoke their own heritage as followers of Christ. Would Christ be so unseeing, so uncaring, of the individual Christians, as Jerry Falwell? No, I do not think so," Brother Joseph concluded. "I would imagine he would say, 'For the least of these are my brothers and sisters.' He would call on all Christians to bear witness to the suffering of the Palestinians."

On another day, I boarded our tour bus in West Jerusalem and rode to the Old City. Leaving the group at Damascus Gate, I walked a few blocks to St. George's Anglican Cathedral and Hostel, where I had an appointment with another Christian, Jonathan Kuttab, an American who had relinquished a flourishing law practice and an easy, somewhat affluent life in the United States in order to return to his native Palestine. Since his return to Jerusalem, Kuttab had become a member of both the West Bank and Israeli Bar Association and served as attorney and a director for Law in the Service of Man, a West Bank affiliate of the International Commission of Jurists.

Arriving early for my appointment, I sat in a church garden of dahlias, roses and chrysanthemums, near a pond of lilies and goldfish. While seated in this oasis of tranquility, I saw a messenger motioning me to follow him, and I walked to Kuttab's office. I found an average-sized man in his late 30s, with handsome, even features, standing behind a desk. He greeted me in a friendly yet businesslike manner, and I began by saying I had come to talk with him not in his role as an attorney, but rather because he was a Christian—a Protestant evangelical Christian.

Could he as an evangelical Christian who had lived in America help me understand the hearts and minds of American pilgrims who will travel to the Land of Christ to visit stone monuments but will not visit the Christians who live here?

"For the evangelical-fundamentalists such as Falwell, the cult of Israel is higher than the teachings of Christ," he answered plainly. "The Christian Zionists such as Falwell pervert the teachings of Christ. Falwell's Zionism is about politics. It has nothing to do with morality, ethics or wrestling with real, serious problems. He tells followers to support Israel. And he tells the American taxpayers to give five billion dollars a year to Israel. He assures his followers that as supporters of Zionism they are on the right side, the 'good' side, the successful, winning side. And he says that they do not ever need to see or hear about any other side.

"Because Falwell has influenced his followers to put the cult of Israel above humanity, few Christian groups come here and seek out Christian organizations. The Christians on such tours practice a folk religion, with a mythology of Israel and prophecy. It negates biblical Christianity.

"The average American finds this mythology very appealing," Kuttab continued. "It is not demanding, nor is it a moral or highly ethical religion. It is a macho religion of the small, ultrapowerful Israel, which is not a sissy. Their God is a cross between Superman and Star Wars, a God who zaps here and there with a fiery, swift sword and destroys all enemies. He is proof for those of weak faith that the Bible is still true and alive. For them, it's almost as if Joshua were in the daily newspaper.

"Christians such as Falwell who hold to a simplistic theology that allows them to see stones but not people exacerbate the problem," Kuttab added. "They provide Israel with carte blanche approval of their militaristic aggressions. Such Christians encourage

Israelis not only to refuse to recognize the Palestinians, but to refuse to withdraw from the West Bank. In fact, Christians such as Falwell provide Israelis with an incentive to expand and take more Arab land and oppress more people because they say God is on their side and Uncle Sam is willing to foot the bill.

"The Israelis know that good, solid red-blooded Christians such as Falwell are with them all the way, regardless of what they do morally or ethically. No matter how oppressive they become, Israelis know the American Christian Zionists are with them and willing to give them weapons and billions of dollars and vote for them in the United Nations."

Falwell prefers not to meet or even see Christians in the Land of Christ because "We, by our mere presence, interfere with his mythology. If he were willing to meet Christians," Kuttab concluded, "he would not need to come to see us, we would go to visit him. I, and countless other Palestinian Christians would welcome the opportunity to visit and talk with all Christians who visit here."

A large portion of Palestinian Christians—perhaps as many as 30,000—continue to live in the Galilee, where Christ had his ministry. When we toured the Galilee, our group could have met with a well-known Christian, Father Elias Chacour, who in his compellingly beautiful autobiography, *Blood Brothers*, details how he felt growing up a Christian in the Land of Christ. Chacour's forebears are among the native Christians who have kept the flame of Christian churches burning since the era of Christ Himself.

Returning on the plane after the 1983 tour, I asked a born again minister, Reverend Clifford, if on his own he had met any Christians while we were touring the Land of Christ.

"One or two," the Reverend Clifford replied.

Tell me truthfully, I said. How many?

"Well," averred the Reverend, "I think I saw one or two from the bus."

TV Evangelist Pat Robertson summed up the general feeling of the New Christian Right when on August 27, 1985 he told syndicated columnist Georgie Anne Geyer:

"There is regard and concern among fundamentalists for the Arabs, but it pales into insignificance compared to (our) feelings toward Jews."

A VISIT
TO LYNCHBURG

One day I boarded a Piedmont airliner in my home city of Washington, D.C., and hardly had gotten settled before the plane had covered the 150 miles to Lynchburg. Nestled in the Piedmont region of rolling hills, Lynchburg, "a city of seven hills," lies at the foot of the Blue Ridge Mountains, in the geographical center of Virginia. Named for John Lynch, an early settler who ran a ferry on the James River, Lynchburg today has a population of about 75,000 people.

After the plane landed, I walked into a modern airport building and quickly spotted two men obviously waiting for an arrival passenger. By previous arrangement made with letters and phone calls, I was there to meet Dr. James Price and Dr. William Goodman, ordained Presbyterian ministers and college professors. Both are in their mid-40s, Price has blondish hair and Goodman has dark hair, a ready smile, and is somewhat more sturdily built than Dr. Price.

The professors have researched Jerry Falwell's life over the past 15 years and have studied his sermons and other remarks made over the past 25 years. I wanted to learn, if possible, when Falwell began his alliance with Israel and how Israel used Falwell—and what Falwell got in return.

"As you came in for the landing, did you see Falwell's plane the Israelis gave him?" Dr. Price asked. Then he pointed to a nearby hanger, with a jet out front. "There it is. It's a Windstream. It's valued anywhere from two and a half to three and a half million dollars. The spare parts came to about a half million. Our source is a pilot, who knows Falwell's pilot. Falwell boasts that he travels as much as 10,000 miles in a week in this jet—recruiting voters for his favored political candidates."

For the next hour, Goodman and Price showed me Falwell's empire, including his mansion, with a huge, sturdy stone wall around it. "Armed security guards are posted at the entrance 24 hours a day," Dr. Price said. We next drove to Thomas Road Baptist church, where Falwell preaches Sunday TV sermons beamed nationwide. And then on to Liberty Baptist College (now Liberty University).

"Falwell very much dominates this town," Dr. Goodman said. Eventually we entered the tree-shaded campus of Lynchburg College—not affiliated with Falwell's domain—where Price and Goodman teach. After parking and walking to one of the buildings, we climbed steps to a book-lined office the two professors share. Over cups of coffee, we continued discussing Falwell, whose ministry, philosophy and basic idea of Christianity differ radically from their own.

Co-authors of *Jerry Falwell: An Unauthorized Profile,* the ministers told me they had learned in their research that prior to 1967 Falwell said preachers should stay out of politics. "He never talked of modern-day Israel at all, prior to 1967," Dr. Price said. To prove his point, Dr. Price shuffled among his papers, and handed me this quote, made by Falwell in 1964:

"Believing the Bible as I do, I would find it impossible to stop preaching the pure saving gospel of Jesus Christ and begin doing anything else, including fighting communism, or participating in civil rights reforms. Preachers are not called on to be politicans but to be soul winners. Nowhere are we commissioned to reform the externals."

After Israel's 1967 military victory, "Falwell changed completely. He entered into politics and became an avid supporter of the Zionist state." My question was obvious: why had Israel's 1967 military victory made a Zionist out of Falwell?

"The stunning Israeli victory made a big impact not only on Falwell, but on a lot of Americans," Dr. Goodman began. "Remember that in 1967, the United States was mired in the Vietnam war. Many felt a sense of defeat, helplessness and discouragement. As Americans we were made acutely aware of our own diminished authority, of no longer being able to police the world or perhaps even our own neighborhoods.

"Many Americans, including Falwell, turned worshipful glances toward Israel, which they viewed as militarily strong and invincible. They gave their unstinting approval to the Israeli takeover of Arab lands because they perceived this conquest as power and righteousness.

"Macho or muscular Christians such as Falwell credited Israeli General Moshe Dayan with this victory over Arab forces and termed him the Miracle Man of the Age, and the Pentagon invited him to visit Vietnam and tell us how to win that war.

"Although that mission failed, Dayan continued to be viewed as a near God," Goodman continued. "No one gave the United States much credit for providing Israel with weapons, technology, billions of dollars and even with American military personnel who aided Israel in that war. Israel won because it had full U.S. backing. But Falwell saw it differently. He said there simply was no way the Israelis could have won, 'had it not been for the intervention of God Almighty.' "

After the defeat of the Social Democratic Labor coalition and the rise of the right-wing Likud bloc, the Israelis, led by Menachem Begin, began to make more consistent use of Falwell, Dr. Price said pointing out that "In 1978, Falwell traveled to Israel on a trip sponsored and paid for by the Israelis and to show his gratitude he planted some trees in what became the Jerry Falwell forest and he was photographed over there, on bended knee.

"In 1979, the Israelis extended another free invitational trip, during a period in which Begin was in a rush to build illegal Jewish colonies throughout the West Bank. Begin had gone to one of the settlements, Elon Moreh, and promised, 'There will be many more Elon Morehs.' And then Begin wanted Falwell to go there and proclaim that God gave the West Bank to the Jews.

"So Falwell, accompanied by his bodyguards and reporters, traveled the road toward the Palestinian town of Nablus and turned off the highway and stood at a cluster of prefabricated houses built by the Jewish settlers. And an Israeli photographer snapped Falwell's photograph with one of the new immigrants, an American named Jed Atlas, from Cherry Hill, New Jersey.

"And with reporters recording his words, Falwell said that God was kind to America only because 'America has been kind to the

Jew.' He added that American Christians must involve themselves politically in such a way 'as to guarantee that America continues to be a friend to the Jew'—that is, the Israelis. Falwell added, 'I believe if we fail to protect Israel, we will cease to be important to God.' " As Dr. Price finished that story, Dr. Goodman picked up:

"Falwell became the first major American political figure to argue that the United States must support Israel not simply for Israel's own sake, but for America's own self-preservation. And he began to boast: 'The Jewish people in America and Israel and all over the world have no dearer friend than Jerry Falwell.' As the 1980 elections approached and his Moral Majority began to get national press attention, Falwell emerged as a prime time media personality, with reporters giving wide coverage to his views on Israel.

"Falwell found many opportunities to tell Americans the fate of the nation stood or fell according to the attitude they took toward Israel. If Americans did not show an unflinching willingness to provide Israel with arms and dollars, Falwell said, America would lose all."

What, I asked,—besides the gift of the jet plane—was Falwell getting in return for all his public relations work for Israel?

"Begin must have given considerable thought to how he could repay Falwell," Jim Price said. "And he decided to present him with one of a very limited number of medals named for Vladimar Zeev Jabotinsky, the right-wing Zionist ideologue—and mentor to Begin. And Begin gave Falwell such a medal at a 1980 gala dinner in New York. If you understand the background of Jabotinsky you can understand why an Israeli leader such as Begin would seek an ally like Falwell. They both understand they have the same goals: they admire power and they advocate ruthlessness in achieving it."

I was sure most Americans had never heard of Jabotinsky. Why did he loom so important?

"Jabotinsky provides a key to understanding why many Israelis such as Begin, Sharon, Shamir and Arens like Falwell and want him as an ally, and also why Falwell looks upon the most militant of the Israeli leaders as heroes," Dr. Price explained.

"Falwell felt honored to recieve a Jabotinsky award because Jabotinsky said power should be your goal, and Falwell thinks like Jabotinsky.

"Jabotinsky held that Jews settling in Palestine should not be held accountable to the laws of man. Anyone who believed in justice, he said, was 'stupid'. No one should trust his neighbor, but rather go fully armed. And Jews should never compromise with the Palestinian Arabs. He insisted on total, unquestioning devotion to the single ideal of establishing a Jewish state. To secure such a state, he urged armed aggression."

In 1923 Jabotinsky founded Betar, a militant youth organization that urged emigration to Palestine. He also started the Jewish Haganah militia, out of which eventually evolved the Israeli army. By 1925 he had formally founded the Revisionist movement as a faction within the World Zionist Organization. Jabotinsky demanded a Kingdom of Israel on both sides of the Jordan River. And urged all Zionist organizations to engage in uncompromising militancy against Arabs.

Falwell's evangelical militancy parallels that of Jabotinsky, explained Dr. Goodman. Falwell claims that "nowhere does the Bible rebuke the bearing of armaments." He scorns the Strategic Arms Limitation Talks and says America's rate of arms production is too slow, calling it a form of "unilateral disarmament." Like Jabotinsky, Falwell has said that "peaceful intentions are acts of stupidity."

"Falwell is the only Gentile ever to receive the Jabotinsky medal. The only difference between his and Jabotinsky's philosophy is that Falwell talks of Christ. But he talks of a militant Christ, a kind of Jabotinsky Christ. Falwell likes Israel not in spite of but because it is militarily aggressive. He admires Israel because it has a big standing army, a big air force, a huge array of tanks and nuclear weapons.

"After pinning the Jabotinsky medal on him, the Israelis utilized Falwell for their purposes to an even greater degree," Dr. Goodman continued. "In 1981, when Begin bombed the reactor at Baghdad, he feared a bad reaction in the United States. For support, he didn't call a Jewish senator or a rabbi—he called Falwell. Begin was worried because we Americans supplied F-16s and bombs to Israel for defensive use and Begin had used them for a pre-emptive strike. So Begin told Falwell, 'Get to work for me.' And Falwell promised he would. Before hanging up, Falwell told Begin:

" 'Mr. Prime Minister, I want to congratulate you for a mission that made us very proud that we manufacture those F-16s.' "

"Whatever military action Israel has taken—or will take—Israel can count on the New Christian Right to support it," Jim Price said. "After Israel bombed the sovereign nation of Iraq, the Moral Majority's Cal Thomas praised the Israelis for what he termed a brillant military operation. Winning in war, Thomas added, was following the Golden Rule—'Whoever has the gold, rules.'

"To my mind, that statement is both unChristian and unAmerican," Price continued. "He is saying that when one loses in war, one has absolutely no rights. This is what the Romans were saying with *vae victis,* woe to the vanquished! But it contrasts with our generous treatment of Germany and Japan after World War II. Though we won that war, we did not assume that we had the right to send settlers in and confiscate German and Japanese territories."

In addition to mustering support for the Israeli strike on Iraq, in what other ways, I asked, had the Israelis made use of Falwell?

"They made good use of him during their 1982 invasion of Lebanon. Falwell had nothing but praise for the invasion," Dr. Goodman said. "He and Cal Thomas of the Moral Majority went over and met Major Haddad, the Israeli puppet in southern Lebanon. Then back in the States, they acted as publicists for the Likud government.

"And when the massacres occurred at the two Palestinian camps, Falwell just mimicked the Israeli line: 'The Israelis were not involved.' And even when the *New York Times* was giving eyewitness accounts of Israeli flares sent up to help the Phalangists go into the camp, Falwell was saying, 'That's just propaganda.' "

To muster national support for the Israeli invasion, Falwell called a meeting with, among others, members of the Reagan administration and former President Richard Nixon. The group met in early August 1983, in Annapolis, Maryland.

Among those attending, Goodman said, were then Secretary of the Interior James Watt; former National Security Counsellor Richard Allen; Frank Shakespeare, a director of the U.S. Information Office; prominent Jewish leader Yehuda Hellman, and New Right leaders Richard Vigurie, Paul Weyrich and Howard Phillips, the founders of the Moral Majority. After the meeting, Falwell said that while none in the group was delegated to speak officially for the White House or other governmental agencies, they were all in "total agreement" in their support of Israel and its invasion of Lebanon.

Price and Goodman told me that in their opinion Falwell and other right-wing Christian leaders gave their "total support" to a foolish military foray that cost Israel 654 deaths with 3,840 wounded. The burden of paying a million dollars a day to sustain the invading and occupying armies wrecked Israel's economy, producing an almost unbelievable inflation rate that drove the consumer price index up to an estimated 1,000 percent and caused countless Israelis to flee the Jewish state for more stable countries, particularly the United States.

Moreover, they concluded, the Israeli bombings and shellings of Beirut and the massacres in the Shatilla and Sabra refugee camps wounded the Jewish state's international reputation almost as much as the war damaged its economy.

A SECOND TOUR
WITH FALWELL

Traveling with Brad

In early 1985, I heard Jerry Falwell announce on TV that he would sponsor another Holy Land tour. I sent the required down payment and asked for further information. And Falwell sent me an expensively produced color brochure. I read details of when I would leave New York, when I would arrive in Tel Aviv, and when I would board a bus and where I would sleep. The brochure, printed in Israel, carried Falwell's words and Falwell's signature. I thought it strange that nowhere in the material did Falwell mention Christ.

On this second tour, I came to a better understanding of why perhaps 40 million evangelical-fundamentalists believe that God favors Jews but not Arabs. One person in particular helped me understand this. His name was Brad, age 35, a native of Georgia, unmarried and traveling alone. A financial manager, a person who helps others plan the most profitable way to invest their money, Brad was well-mannered and neatly dressed.

Unlike many religious zealots who must argue because they cannot discuss, Brad was patient and spoke in a soft yet resonant voice. He seemed to be flattered I would seek his opinions, and in spite of or even because of the differences in our ages and life experiences we were developing a friendship, or at least a pattern of seeking one another out to share a meal or a bus ride.

With a full head of red hair and neatly cropped mustache and beard, Brad seemed a deadringer for the Atlanta syndicated columnist Lewis Grizzard, who once bragged he was the "quintessential southern male." Brad had read all of Grizzard's books, including *If Love Were Oil, I'd Be About a Quart Low*, and, on the subject of his open-heart surgery, *They Tore Out My Heart and Stomped That Sucker Flat*.

"We think alike," Brad said. "We both think that in a marriage someone has to be boss—and it's got to be the male." And Brad added, "He thinks homos are sick. And so do I."

It was surprising, in retrospect, how many subjects we discussed. But generally we discussed the Bible and Brad's church affiliation, which was Assemblies of God or Pentecostal, the fastest growing segment in Christianity today.

It was while he was in college, Brad said, that he experienced a failed marriage and a time of heavy drinking. He entered a period of spiritual distress, and in these dark days—where he had even contemplated suicide—he had turned to Christ. For the first time he had a focus and meaning to his life. Previously he had been a loner, unable to express his emotions, but among other born again Christians and particularly charismatics, he was able to express some of his deepest feelings—and even to shout these emotions. He now felt a sense of belonging, of not being alone, of being part of an expansive community of other men and women who felt and thought as he did.

One day Brad and I were on our tour bus and our conversation had lapsed into a long silence when Brad somewhat suddenly said:

"I just wish I had been born a Jew!"

It was a softly-muted, yet fervent confession. As he spoke, his body moved with a visible shiver—as if a cold wind had blown over him. His sharing of a religious conviction left me with no ready response. My mind flitted back to Japan, when, shortly after World War II, I was riding a crowded Tokyo subway with a young Japanese woman friend who suddenly exclaimed, "Oh! I wish I had been born a man!" When I had asked why, she explained her father did not view females as good as males. I thought her regret at not being one of the "chosen" might provide a key to Brad's pronouncement.

With this in mind, I asked Brad if God viewed non-Jews as less good than Jews—because Jews were His Chosen People?

"Yes, definitely," he replied, adding that when God made the universe, He gave His special blessing to the Jews. For this reason, Jews were "different and better" than non-Jews.

"First of all, He wanted the Jews to take possession of the Holy Land. As to who has title deed to the Holy Land, God settled that question. God promised all of this land to the Jews." Then naming Genesis 12 as source for "the original blessing," Brad quoted verses that go:

"The Lord said to Abram, 'Go from your country . . . to the land that I will show you, and I will make of you a great nation . . . and by you shall all the families of the earth be blessed.' "

Brad also quoted from Genesis 15:18, "Unto thy seed have I given this land, from the river of Egypt unto the great river, the river Euphrates."

"There is some question as to what is meant by 'the river of Egypt', since there is a stream bed now known as the Wadi El Arish which has been known also in times past as 'the river of Egypt,' " Brad said. "But I believe that 'the river of Egypt' is no less than the Nile. And if that is true, then parts of Egypt—that is, the Sinai and some additional land now controlled by Egypt—fall within the divinely-given title given to Abraham.

"I think it would be evil in the sight of God for American officials to consider sitting down to any 'peace process' that would take one square foot of land away from the people who hold the oldest title deed to property known to mankind," Brad said.

If indeed a universal God deeded land only to a few, did this not smack of particularism, favoritism and discrimination?

"God did not promise the land to the non-Jews, the Arabs," Brad answered.

Did Brad believe, I asked, that the modern political entity called Israel—created after the holocaust in Nazi Germany—is the same as the ancient entity we read about in the Bible?

"Yes," said Brad. "The Hebrew nation established 3,000 or more years ago and the Jewish state created in 1948 are the same. The Bible says Israel will be recreated—and it was. This convinces me that the Bible is true."

And were the people who in recent years moved into Palestine from Europe—Westerners such as Menachem Begin from Poland and Golda Meir from the United States—were they the same people as the Semites who lived in Palestine over 3,000 years ago? Those Semites, I suggested, were Orientals.

"The Jews," Brad replied, "are all one race of people."

I suggested that a Jew living in Yemen would be considered an Oriental and a Jew living in France would be a Caucasian, while the Ethiopian black Falashas would be Negroid.

"No, all Jews are one race—and have been since Abraham," he

maintained. Brad insisted that the world "consists only of two races of people, Jews and non-Jews. And God always has His eye on His people, the Jews."

Earlier on, I recalled, Brad had said he felt so strongly on this subject that he wished he had been born a Jew. I had no idea whether he was sentimentalizing out of piety, or whether he truly desired to don a yarmulke and worship God in a synagogue. In either event, Brad tended to resemble and identify with pre-Christian messianic Judaism. In this respect, he was like some of the Pilgrims, who also felt in their heart of hearts they were Jewish. Many prayed in Hebrew and utilized the Mosaic law in their daily lives. They felt their own history the continuation of the early Hebrews, their own lives the reflection, their own achievements the fulfillment of the experience of a Palestine of so many centuries before.

"Gentile," Brad told me, means "pagan" and he added, "There are only Jews and pagans. And I don't want to be a pagan."

Palestine, he had said, was a land selected by God for His Chosen People, and Brad, if he wished to convert to Judaism, would have the right to Palestinian land as did Ben-Gurion, Begin, Shamir, Golda Meir, Bobby Brown and other immigrants. Under the Jewish Law of Return, any immigrating Jew (defined as one with a Jewish mother or a convert to Judaism) is granted citizenship.

Since Brad strongly identified with the Jews as a Chosen People and with the land we traversed not as a spiritual Zion—an allegorical haven for all those who believe in one God—but rather as a piece of real estate exclusively for Jews, I wondered if he might feel more comfortable practicing Judaism rather than Christianity. Had he considered converting to Judaism?

"No," he said, "Our duties as Christians are to be a blessing to the Jews, to support them in all their endeavors, to stand with them."

For Brad, the pronouncements to bless Israel are living words, as real as "thou shalt not kill" or "thou shalt not steal." When and where and under what circumstances the words were composed are unimportant to him. The early blessings and curses written down by an early Oriental tribal people, Brad insisted, can and do extend to our shores.

Brad believed that the term "chosenness" meant God wanted only Jews to live in the Holy Land. In this respect, he was unlike the Hebrew prophets, who regarded "chosenness" as requiring responsibility and not granting special privilege in real estate claims or sovereignty.

"Israel was right to invade Lebanon," Brad said to me. "If they took Arab lands, they had the God-given right to do so. And they should have taken more!"

Was it in the Bible, I asked Brad, that God wanted Israel to invade Lebanon—and precisely at the time they did?

"Yes, it's part of prophecy," he said. "You see the Palestinians who fought against the Israelis in Lebanon were part of the PLO. And they used weapons provided by the Soviet Union, so the invasion was a proxy war with the Soviet Union, with the PLO fighting in place of the Russians. So the defeat of the PLO was a defeat for the Russians.

"The Bible also shows," Brad continued, "that we should momentarily expect an attack on Israel by Russia and a confederation of Arab leaders. We can be confident that this attack is coming because it is prophesied in the books of Daniel and Ezekiel."

Like many Christians on the tour, Brad carried a personal Bible with him, often referring to it when our group waited for a bus or a meal. Brad's Bible was a Scofield Bible. One evening, Brad and I looked over his Bible. He turned to the 38th chapter of Ezekiel, with a heading—provided by Scofield—entitled "The prophecy against Gog." The chapter begins, "And the word of the Lord came unto me, saying, Son of man, set thy face against Gog, the land of Magog, the chief prince of Meshech and Tubal, and prophesy against him."

Then following the biblical scripture, we read Scofield's interpretation. In a footnote identifying Gog, Scofield wrote "That the primary reference is to the northern (European) powers, headed up by Russia, all agree."(Scofield does not amplify who is included in the term "all".)

" 'Gog' is the prince,' 'Magog' is his land,' " Scofield writes. "The reference to Meshech and Tubal (Moscow and Tobolsk) is a clear mark of identification. Russia and the northern powers have been the latest persecutors of dispersed Israel . . ." They (Russia and cohorts) will meet destruction, Scofield writes, adding that the whole prophecy "belongs to the battle of Armageddon."

As Brad and I studied the text, it became plain that Gog was described as a 'chief prince'. The terms used in Ezekiel 38 for chief prince are *nasi'* (meaning prince) and *rosh* (meaning head or chief).

That comes out "chief prince," I said. How did Brad get Russia out of it?

"*Rosh* should not be used as a descriptive noun qualifying the word prince, but rather as a proper name. So this makes the phrase *nasi' rosh* means 'prince of *rosh*', which gives us the term, 'prince of Russia'."

Since he was convinced that *rosh* meant Russia, we therefore must fight *rosh*, that is, Russia?

"Yes, definitely," he replied.

Brad was not impressed by my pointing out that the author of the phrase about *rosh* did not speak or understand English (Russia is an English word) and moreover that back in those days there was no Russia, anyway. In any case, what seemed of greater interest to me at the moment was Brad's reverence for Scofield. Brad, as a born again Christian, believed the Bible was infallible, without error. Since Scofield had written his interpretation of Scripture in the Bible, at least in the Bible Brad carried, Brad believed every word penned by Scofield. He accepted Scofield's words as literally and completely as he accepted the words of Jesus Christ.

What, in essence, I asked Brad, did Scofield—and dispensationalism—teach? How would Brad define his own belief system of dispensationalism?

"We believe that history is now unfolding to a seventh and climactic time period: the establishment of Christ's kingdom, where Christ will reign from Jerusalem for 1,000 years. All Jews will have converted to Christ and will participate in the administration of Christ's millennial kingdom—a literal kingdom on earth with its headquarters in Jerusalem."

Asked to name the events that must precede the seventh and climactic time period, Brad began:

"First, the return of the Jews to the land of Palestine. Second, the establishment of a Jewish state."

Because Brad believes the biblical Israel of millennia past to be the dateline for all history, past, present and future, he says he "rejoiced" when a new political entity was carved out of Palestinian soil in 1947 and given the old biblical name of Israel, to associate it in the minds of people today with the religious Zion of Scripture.

"The creation of a new Israel with the Jews reestablished in the land promised them by God gives us incontrovertible proof that God's divine plan is in operation and the Second Coming of our Savior is assured. For me, the creation of the state of Israel is the most momentous event of modern history. It represents the first step toward the beginning of the End Times.

"God gave us another signal in 1967, when He gave victory to the Israelis over the Arabs and allowed the Jews to take the biblical lands of Judea and Samaria as well as to gain military control over the old city of Jerusalem. For the first time in more than 2,000 years the Jews were in control of Jerusalem. Again I felt a new thrill and a renewed faith in the accuracy and validity of the Bible.

"The third necessary event is the preaching of the gospel to all nations, including Israel. With short-wave radios and television, the message of Christ has been spread around the world. We now have 40,000 evangelical foreign missionaries around the world. The word has gone to all nations.

"I expect the fourth event, the Rapture or lifting up of the church, to occur any day. Then comes the fifth event, the Tribulation, a period of great suffering. For seven years those who are not Raptured will undergo great persecution. They will be waging wars—led by a leader called the Antichrist. Then comes the sixth event—the Battle of Armageddon."

Brad paused and reflected a moment. While he said he was happy the Jews had returned to Palestine and that the state of Israel had been created, he felt the Jews had not entirely completed their mission: "Jews today must redeem all of the land God gave to the Hebrews."

When he used the word *redeem* the land, what exactly did ne mean?

"The Jews must own all of the land promised by God before Christ can return." He added, "The Arabs have to leave this land because this land belongs only to the Jews. God gave all of this land to the Jews."

A Visit to
a Holy Mount

On the 1985 tour, I became acquainted with Owen, 59, a retired Army major. Slightly built, about five feet, five inches tall, he stood erect and had a pleasant if rather shy smile. Well dressed and with a full head of sandy hair, he looked younger than his age. He had served in Europe during World War II and later for a number of years in Japan. Like Clyde, whom I met on the 1983 trip, Owen was a widower. His wife recently had undergone a long and agonizing death from cancer, and he had faithfully cared for her. He now lived alone in a northern town of Nebraska.

I enjoyed spending time with Owen. He was a walker and we often rose early to get in a couple of miles of hiking. Sometimes we walked in the evenings, after dinner. He and I had both traveled and lived in many of the same places, and we enjoyed reminiscing about days in Rome, Paris and Vienna—about skiing in Bavaria and climbing Mt. Fuji in Japan.

Most of all, however, we talked about religion, the most important aspect of his life. Since his retirement, Owen had gone into the real estate business. Having made good money, he was a big contributor—in the tens of thousands of dollars, I learned—to Jerry Falwell as well as to other TV evangelicals, including Pat Robertson. Like Brad and Clyde and Mona and others I had previously met, Owen carried a Scofield Bible and used it as an infallible guide to interpret today's events.

One day our group went to the old walled city of Jerusalem. As we entered Damascus Gate and passed along cobblestone corridors, I could easily imagine Jesus having walked a similar route. In the midst of a rapidly changing environment, the old walled city, guarding layer upon layer of history and conflict, provides the stellar

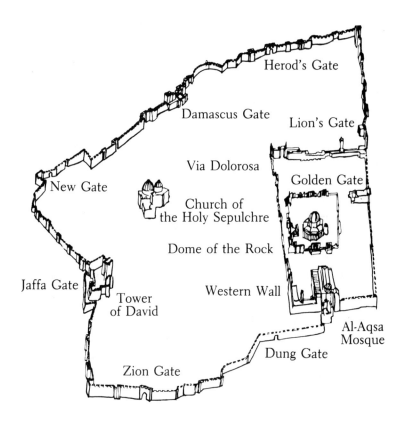

Herod's Gate

Damascus Gate

Lion's Gate

Via Dolorosa

New Gate

Golden Gate

Church of
the Holy Sepulchre

Dome of the Rock

Jaffa Gate

Western Wall

Tower
of David

Al-Aqsa
Mosque

Zion Gate

Dung Gate

Jerusalem (Old City)

For most of its long history, Jerusalem has been a predominantly
Arab city. Within the walls of the old city are shrines for three faiths:
Islam's Dome of the Rock and Al-Aqsa Mosque (on raised platform
grounds); Judaism's Western Wall and Christianity's Church of the
Holy Sepulchre. The old city is home for 25,000 people, many of
whose forebears have lived there since before the time of Christ.

attraction for tourists and remains home for 25,000 people, the overwhelming majority of them Palestinian Muslims and Christians.

I was walking alongside Owen as our group approached the large Muslim grounds called Haram al-Sharif, or Noble Sanctuary, which encloses the Dome of the Rock and Al-Aqsa Mosque. Both these edifices, on raised platform grounds, are generally referred to simply as "the mosque" and represent Jerusalem's most holy Islamic shrine.

We stood on lower ground below the mosque and faced the Western Wall, a 200-foot-high and 1,600-foot-long block of huge white stones, believed to be the only remnant of the second Jewish temple.

"There—" our guide said, pointing upward toward the Dome of the Rock and Al-Aqsa mosque—"we will build our third temple. We have all the plans drawn for the temple. Even the building materials are ready. They are hidden in a secret place. There are several shops where Israelis work, making the artifacts we will use in the new temple. One Israeli is weaving the pure linen that will be used for garments of the priests of the temple." He paused and then added:

"In a religious school called Yeshiva Ateret Cohanim—the Crown of the Priests—located near where we are standing, rabbis are teaching young men how to make animal sacrifice."

A woman in our group, Mary Lou, a computer specialist, was startled to hear the Israelis wanted to return to the rites of the old Solomonic sacrificial altar of the temple.

"You are going back to animal sacrifice?" she asked. "Why?"

"It was done in the First and Second Temples," our Israeli guide said. "And we do not wish to change the practices. Our sages teach that neglecting to study the details of temple service is a sin."

As we left the site, I remarked to Owen that our Israeli guide had said a temple would be built on the Dome of the Rock site. But he said nothing about the Muslim shrines.

"They will be destroyed," said Owen. "You know it's in the Bible that the temple must be rebuilt. And there's no other place for it except on that one area. You find that in the law of Moses."

Did it not seem possible, I asked, that the Scripture about building a temple would relate to the time in which it was written— rather than to events in the 20th century?

"No, it is related to the End Time," Owen said. "The Bible tells us that in the End Times the Jews will have renewed their animal sacrifice."

In other words, I said, a temple must be built so that the Jews can resume their animal sacrifices?

"Yes," said Owen, quoting Ezekiel 44:29 to prove his point.

Was Owen convinced that Jews, aided by Christians, should destroy the mosque, build a temple and reinstate the killing of animals in the temple—all in order to please God?

That, said Owen, was the way it had to be. It was in the Bible.

Does the building of the temple, I asked, fit into any time sequence?

"Yes," he said."We think it will be the next step in the events leading to the return of our Lord. As far as its being a large temple, the Bible doesn't tell us that. All it tells us is that there will be a renewal of sacrifices. And that would require a relatively small building."

He was referring to animal sacrifice within the temple? Was it not atavistic to go back to animal sacrifice?

"It is, but that is what the Bible predicts," Owen said. "Now the people who are going to do it are not Christians but Orthodox Jews. Of course the Old Testament made out a very specific formula for it, and they can't carry it out without a temple and they were observing it until 70 A.D. And when they have a temple they will have some Orthodox Jews who will kill the sheep or oxen in the temple, as a sacrifice to God."

As Owen talked of animal sacrifice—a step in his dispensationalist belief system he felt necessary for his own spiritual maturity—he seemed to block from his awareness the fact that Muslim shrines stood on the site where he wanted a temple to stand.

Would he take the time, I ventured to ask—and I mentioned a time when our group would be given a couple of hours in our schedule for shopping—to visit the Muslim shrines with me? He registered surprise and even disappointment that I would consider going to shrines built by "heathens." He added that he would not go and I should not either.

Nevertheless, when others, including Owen, went shopping, I walked alone to the Muslim Noble Sanctuary or Haram al-Sharif.

It was a Friday, a Muslim Holy Day, and walking to Al-Aqsa, I was
aware I was moving among thousands of Arabs as they made their
way along Jerusalem's cobblestone corridors to pray at the mosque.

As Paris has for thousands of years been predominantly and
overwhelmingly Gallic or French, so Jerusalem throughout its long
history has been predominantly and overwhelmingly Arab. Amorites
came to the holy site 4,000 to 5,000 years ago, then Canaanites from
Canaan. All of this early history predates the arrival of the Hebrews
by many centuries. And when a tribe of Hebrews, one of many
tribes in the area, did arrive, they stayed for less than 400 years.
And they, too, like many before and after, were defeated. And 2,000
years ago they were driven out. It was what we in the West called
the Orient in our history books, and it remains so.

I continued my walk, and near the Western, or Wailing, Wall—
where Owen and I had once talked—I climbed steps to enter onto
raised platform grounds on a man-made plateau. The Noble Sanctuary or Haram al-Sharif grounds measure 40 acres and cover one-
sixth of the old walled city.

For 1,300 years, continuously from the seventh century to the
present, except for an 88-year Christian Crusader period, the
Muslims have maintained the "Sacred Place" of Jerusalem, ruling
it through the Muslim Supreme Council and its executive arm,
called the Islamic awqaf, which control not only Haram al-Sharif
but 35 other mosques, many cemeteries and other Islamic religious
sites within the old city.

In 1967, the Israelis seized military control of the old city. Wanting space for a large plaza in front of the Wailing Wall, they bull-
dozed the Arab Moghrabi quarter—so named for an area in Arab
North Africa—and evicted an estimated 5,000 to 6,000 people living in this quarter. The obliteration of homes, schools and mosques
in the area triggered the concern of the British School of Archaeology in Jerusalem. Alarmed about the safety of major Islamic
monuments around Haram al-Sharif, the school began a survey of
1,300 years of Islamic architecture and pinpointed monuments that
should be preserved.

In their survey, the British School lists some 30 Islamic
monuments in the old city from the Umayyad, Abbasid, Farimid
and Ayyubid periods, 79 from the Mamluk period and 37 Ottoman

buildings of note. The Islamic awqaf authorities have responsibility for most of these buildings, which create the present shape and skyline of much of the old city and are therefore of great importance in determining its character.

Walking alone in the old city, I make my way toward the magnificent Dome of the Rock, one of the most beautiful shrines in all of the world—often compared in its beauty with the Taj Mahal. It was constructed—in 685—by the order of Abdul-Malek Ibn Marwan, the Umayyad Caliph of Damascus. To visit this shrine, an octagonal masterpiece fashioned with blue and green tiles that glisten in the Mediterranean light, I step onto a raised, terrace-like platform, surrounded by pillars with stairways on every side. I look above to an incredibly large yet graceful gilded dome.

At the entrance of the Dome of the Rock, I, along with dozens of other visitors from around the world, remove my shoes and once inside walk on ancient, richly textured Oriental rugs. After a half-dozen steps I reach a guardrail framing a large boulder. I am startled by the unexpected dimensions of the rock. I see a large mass of mineral matter from the earth's crust, a boulder like many others I have seen in countless regions of the earth. The rock, which rises above the ground to my shoulders and covers an area half the size of a tennis court, dominates the entire space within the shrine.

Jerusalem's most beautiful architectural gem was built for one sole purpose: to protect and enhance the huge rock. I see only mineral matter, but Muslims looking at the rock see eternity, a foundation stone of the universe, the center of the world and a focus of their faith.

The prophet Mohammed believed the great rock had its origins in Paradise. And today about 800 million Muslims believe that from this sacred rock Mohammed was transported by God to heaven.

Nearby stands Al-Aqsa Mosque, with its vast courtyard, where 10,000 Muslims may gather to pray. On entering the mosque the first time, I note the beauty of more than a hundred stained-glass windows fashioned in stylized, colorful arabesque designs. Again, as in the Dome of the Rock, I walk on luxurious handwoven carpets. I am impressed by the mosque's stately architecture and dignity, unmarred by over-scheduled tourists following leaders who shout details of holy sites through amplified mouthpieces. I see only individuals at prayer. I kneel, remain quiet and after awhile, leave.

Having visited Haram al-Sharif, I gleaned a sense of how deeply the Muslims—now so numerous they are every fifth person in the world—cherish their holy shrines. I feared that if Jewish fanatics, aided by Christian fanatics, in a holy war, or jihad, against the Muslims destroyed the Muslims' most holy Jerusalem shrines, they might easily trigger World War III and a nuclear holocaust.

I had talked at length with Owen about this. But whenever I reminded him that the Muslim shrines were there and deeply meaningful to the Muslims, he said that was "inconsequential."

I wondered: was his thinking truly representative of Christian fundamentalism? Were the evangelical-fundamentalist leaders unaware, unmindful or even scornful of the feelings of almost a billion Muslims in 60 countries around the world?

The Hebrews built their first temple in Jerusalem in 950 B.C. and this temple was destroyed in 587-6 B.C. by the Babylonians. They built a second temple in 515 B.C. and this was destroyed in A.D. 70 by the Romans. Archaeologists have not found any artifacts indicating where either the first or the second temple was located, but many presume that they were built on the site where Islam's most holy shrines are now located.

Most Christians today believe that when Christ was here on earth He taught that each of us should build "a temple of goodness" within our souls. In John 2:20-21, Jesus speaks of its having taken 46 years to build a temple, and asks, "Will you raise it up in three days?" The Scripture adds, "But he spoke of the temple of his body." And in John 4:7-24, we read the story of the woman of Samaria who draws water from a well for Jesus. When she asks Him about worship on a holy mountain and at the temple in Jerusalem, Jesus replies:

"Woman, believe me, the hour is coming when neither on this mountain nor in Jerusalem will you worship the Father . . . The hour is coming, and now is, when the true worshipers will worship the Father in spirit and truth, for such the Father seeks to worship him."

Christian dispensationalists insist, however, that God wants more than a spiritual temple, that He demands an actual temple of stone and mortar, and on the very site of Muslim shrines.

Of my concerns about the dangers inherent in the plot to destroy Islam's holy shrines, Owen had answered that Christians need not do it, but he was sure the shrines would be destroyed. His logic was simple—what will be will be because God wills it.

"I say Jewish terrorists will blow up the Islamic holy place and this will provoke the Muslim world into a cataclysmic holy war with Israel that will force the Messiah to intervene. The Jews think He will be coming for the first time, and we Christians know it will be His second visit," Owen told me, adding simply, "Yes, there definitely must be a third Jewish temple."

This is also what Hal Lindsey says. In *The Late Great Planet Earth* he writes, "There remains but one more event to completely set the stage for Israel's part in the last great act of her historical drama. This is to rebuild the ancient Temple of worship upon its old site. There is only one place that this Temple can be built, according to the law of Moses. This is upon Mt. Moriah. It is there that the two previous Temples were built."

Provoking a Holy War

Before going on the second Falwell-sponsored tour, I talked with Terry Reisenhoover, a native of Oklahoma, who heads an organization called the Jerusalem Temple Foundation, which he and other Americans established to aid Jewish terrorists destroy the Muslim shrines.

In his mid-40s, short, rotund, and balding, Reisenhoover lived in California where he headed the Alaska Land Leasing Company and Sunbelt Homes. Reisenhoover also formed an exploration company specifically to search for oil in the portion of occupied Palestine called the West Bank.

A born again Christian, Reisenhoover is blessed with a fine tenor voice. In White House gatherings of right-wing Christians, he has been a featured soloist, accompanied on the violin by Shony Braun, an associate in schemes for buying up West Bank Palestinian land. A survivor of the Auschwitz concentration camp, he is today an American-Israeli dual citizen.

Reisenhoover views himself as "the new Nehemiah." As the biblical Nehemiah was dispatched to rebuild Jerusalem, so he believes he is called to rebuild a temple even though he is a Gentile and most Jews, Christians and Muslims would disapprove of his program and tactics.

To move tax-free dollars to Israel from wealthy American donors, Reisenhoover helped organize and in 1985 served as Chairman for the American Forum for Jewish-Christian Cooperation. He was assisted by Douglas Krieger as executive director, and an American rabbi, David Ben-Ami, closely linked with Ariel Sharon, as president.

Additionally Reisenhoover served as chairman of the board for the Jerusalem Temple Foundation, and as his international secretary for this foundation he chose Stanley Goldfoot, regarded by some people as a terrorist. Goldfoot, who emigrated in the 1930s from South Africa to Palestine, became a member of the notorious Stern gang, which shocked the world with its massacres of Arab men, women and children. Such figures as David Ben-Gurion denounced the gang as Nazis and outlawed them.

Goldfoot, according to the Israeli newspaper *Davar*, placed a bomb on July 22, 1946, in Jerusalem's King David Hotel that destroyed a wing of the hotel housing the British Mandate secretariat and part of the military headquarters. The operation killed about 100 British and other officials and, as the Zionists planned, hastened the day the British left Palestine.

Although Stanley Goldfoot, one of the Israelis most intent on building a temple, does not believe in God or sacred aspects of the Old Testament, he and his associates justify their militant plans to take over Haram al-Sharif by quoting Scripture. They say that God gave the Holy Land to Abraham and his son Jacob and not to another of Abraham's sons named Ishmael. As Goldfoot's deputy Yisrael Meida, a member of the ultra right-wing Tehiya party, explains:

"It is all a matter of sovereignty. He who controls the Temple Mount, controls Jerusalem. And he who controls Jerusalem, controls the land of Israel.

"This is the land of Israel and not the land of Ishmael," Meida continues, adding that even if militant Jews don't succeed in expelling the Arabs from Haram al-Sharif in his generation, "it will be done in the next generation. King David bought the Temple Mount for good money and we have a *kushan* (certificate of ownership, that is, the Bible) for it."

Christians such as Reisenhoover admire such talk. And many of them view Goldfoot with an awe that resembles a six-year-old kid's admiration for the biggest bully on the block. "Goldfoot is a very solid, legitimate terrorist," said Reisenhoover in describing Goldfoot's qualifications for building a temple.

In Jerusalem, I had sought to learn more about the Jerusalem Temple Foundation from George Giacumakis, who for many years headed the Institute for Holy Land Studies, a long established American-run evangelical school for studies in archaeology and theology. I set an appointment with Giacumakis, a Greek American with dark eyes and cultivated charm. After we visited casually over coffee, I asked if he might help me arrange an interview with Goldfoot. In response, Giacumakis dropped his head in both hands, as one does on hearing a disaster.

"Oh, no. You don't want to meet him. He goes back to the Irgun!" Then raising his head and waving an arm toward the King David Hotel, he added, "Stanley Goldfoot was in charge of that operation. He will not stop at anything. His idea is to rebuild the temple, and if that means violence, then he will not hesitate to use violence." Giacumakis paused and then assured me that while he himself did not believe in violence, "If they do destroy the mosque and the temple is there, that does not mean I will not support it."

Sponsored by Terry Reisenhoover, Goldfoot has made several trips to the United States, where he spoke on religious radio and TV stations and in Protestant churches, asking Christians for donations but not mentioning that a mosque sits on the site where he contemplates a temple.

Goldfoot admits that he has received money from the International Christian Embassy, whose funding, many believe, comes from South Africa. Asked about the Goldfoot statement that he had received money from his organization, Christian Embassy spokesman Jan Willem van der Hoeven denied that they are directly involved in the temple construction efforts. Rather, he said, when supporters volunteer to give money for building a temple, he directs them to Goldfoot. The embassy has, however, made a cassette it sells for $5.00 that features a taped message about plans to build a temple on Haram al-Sharif. Van der Hoeven is one of the speakers on the tape.

I heard more about Goldfoot from one of his many Christian admirers, the Reverend James E. DeLoach of Houston's Second Baptist Church. I first talked by telephone with the pastor one day in late 1983 when I was in Houston. On the phone, he was low-key, quiet-spoken, genial and, like many Texans, in no rush. I noted he used a Dale Carnegie technique of repeating one's first name often and pronouncing it in a way one likes to hear. We had never met and I knew nothing about him and he did not know anything about me, except that I had told him I was a writer and had talked

with Terry Reisenhoover—and that Reisenhoover had given me
his name and suggested I call him.

A few weeks later, I was back home in Washington, D.C., and
DeLoach arrived in town for a religious conference. He called telling me he was at the Sheraton Hotel. I said that I lived "next door,"
and I invited him by for a visit. Shortly a bell rang and I opened
the door to see a bald-headed man with a kind face—a man who
could be my brother, uncle or a helpful neighbor. We soon were
seated, and he began telling me about Goldfoot.

"I know Stanley very very well. We're good friends. He's just
real unusual . . . he's a loyalist, a Zionist, and a very strong person."

And, I asked, Goldfoot wants to see the mosque destroyed?

"Well, now, naturally every Jew that I know would like to see
the mosque gone. But they tell me that they believe it will be
destroyed by an act of God, by an earthquake or something—so
that they won't even have to do it."

Why, as a Christian, was he working to build a Jewish temple?

"My interest in the Jerusalem Temple Foundation is not
primarily an interest in the temple. My interest primarily is in
religious freedom. The thing that troubles me more than anything
else is that in all the land of Israel, one of the most sacred sites
for Christians and Jews and Muslims is the Temple Mount area
and the Muslims consistently have forbidden Christians to have
worship services on the very hill and the very place where the
church was born.

"Now, in America, we believe in Christian freedom, and that
means that we believe in religious freedom. That means that any
religious person has a right to practice his religion under the full
protection of the law—*anyone*, evangelical Christian, Jew, Roman
Catholic, Muslim—whatever. But in Jerusalem, at one of the most
sacred places, Christians are not permitted to pray."

DeLoach talked for more than an hour, devoting about 15
minutes to a Christian's right to a freedom to pray—all of which
he allowed me to tape record. And while none of it made much
sense to me, I heard him to the finish, with all his references to
chapters and verses that he thought to include. I refrained from
interrupting him, but I could scarcely believe Pastor DeLoach along
with Terry Reisenhoover, Doug Krieger and other dispensationalists

were raising $100 million—he had said that was their annual yearly goal—to gain the right to pray at a certain shrine in Jerusalem. One may, of course, pray anywhere, and at no cost.

"Other than this freedom to pray, I have absolutely no interest in the temple," DeLoach insisted. Asked if Terry Reisenhoover's reason for building a temple was the same as his, he said, "I think that Terry maybe . . . Terry . . . I can't really speak on that, I can't really. Terry and I have discussed this on occasions, and I'm not really clear as to what Terry really believes."

Despite Reisenhoover's being in charge of a $100 million annual fund raising project, DeLoach did not understand his associate's motives?

"Well, Terry has been blessed by God with a gift of making money. And he is also a very generous person with his gifts." As an example of his generosity, Reisenhoover produced the money, DeLoach said, used to pay lawyers who gained freedom for 29 Israeli militants who in 1983 stormed Al-Aqsa Mosque, were jailed and put on trial.

"It cost us quite a lot of money to get their freedom," DeLoach told me.

The pastor also indicated that Reisenhoover's group is providing support for the Ateret Cohanim yeshiva that prepares students such as 27-year old Mattityahu Hacohen Dan—a *cohen*, or priest—for service in a Temple they hope will be built. Twenty-five of the yeshiva's young scholars devote at least one hour every day, and an additional afternoon every week, to concentrated study of the laws of temple worship. Three other yeshivas as well teach their students how to burn incense and follow other laws dealing with the temple practice, including how to offer animal sacrifices.

"Two of the young Israelis who study animal sacrifices were guests in my home for several weeks," Pastor DeLoach told me.

Before DeLoach left my apartment that day I asked him one final question: What if the Jewish terrorists he supports are successful and they destroy the Dome of the Rock and Al-Aqsa and this triggers World War III and a nuclear holocaust—would he and Reisenhoover not be responsible?

"No," he said—because what they are doing was "God's will."

In addition to Reisenhoover, Krieger and DeLoach, other

Jerusalem Temple Foundation directors include Dr. Charles E. Monroe, president of the Center of Judeo-Christian Studies in Poway, California, and Dr. Hilton Sutton, an evangelical-fundamentalist preacher and chairman of an organization with Israeli ties called Mission to America, located in Humble, Texas.

Dr. Lambert Dolphin, a top-ranking scientist with the Stanford Research Institute (SRI) in California, does not serve on the Jerusalem Temple Foundation, but he nevertheless maintains the closest of ties with its leaders and he adheres to its goals. Dolphin, Pastor DeLoach told me, is the innovator of a plan "that uses ground search radar sort of like an x-ray machine for archaeological purposes. His ground search radar has a great deal of validity."

I first began a correspondence with Dr. Dolphin in April, 1983, and because we wrote each other with some frequency, occasionally talked on the telephone and exchanged Christmas cards, we got on a first-name basis.

He sent me packages of his material, some of it highly technical and some of it personal, such as a pamphlet describing his born again experience. He does not detail specifically his past imperfect years but one might assume he was in a fast lane, intent on gaining money rather than saving his soul. Then he found Christ. Finding Christ in his case also meant accepting the dispensationalists' belief that many events connected with his Christian growth must occur in Israel, and that America therefore should give 100 percent support to that nation. Otherwise there might not be an Israel, and without Israel his dispensational belief system would crumble.

Dolphin, who probably earns a six-figure salary at the prestigious Stanford Research Institute, has provided dispensationalist clients of SRI with a synopsis of why he believes they should help the Jews build a temple. His pamphlet "Geophysical Methods for Archaeological Surveys in Israel," describes how an area can be explored archaeologically—by aerial photography, thermal infrared imagery, ground penetration radar and seismic sounding—without actually digging.

In many of the proposed archaeological digs, heavy equipment is required. Dolphin explains that he would need the cooperation of those in control of the area, in this case the Muslim Supreme Council, which is r ot likely to agree to any such project. Dolphin points out that with airborne radar it would not be necessary to inform the Muslims that the activity was taking place.

In another pamphlet, Dolphin notes that on the holy mount, where three religions lay claim to a sacred plot of land of 100,000 square meters—"digging is difficult and remote sensing is to be preferred." In asking for funds—to be sent to Stanley Goldfoot— Dolphin indicates that a single field season and follow-up program can cost from "low six figures to mid-seven figures," that is, anywhere from a couple of hundred thousand to several million dollars.

In 1983, Lambert Dolphin spent several weeks in Jerusalem on a mission connected with the Jerusalem Temple Foundation and partially funded by the Reverend Chuck Smith's Calvary Baptist Church in Santa Ana, California. Dolphin intended using his ground search radar equipment to probe Haram al-Sharif for any evidence that a temple had once been there. Thus far, no one has found any such evidence.

In Jerusalem, however, after he began "x-raying" Haram al-Sharif, including the space over, around and under the Dome of the Rock and Al-Aqsa Mosque, the religious Muslims who control the area objected to his probes. Faced with stiff opposition from religious Jews, who believe it wrong to disturb the holy site, as well as religious Muslims, Dolphin packed his gear and returned to California.

Nationalistic minded Zionists over the years have applied unrelenting pressure on successive Israeli governments to assume sovereignty over the Haram al-Sharif. The Israeli parliament as well as the Israeli Supreme Court, fearful that the destruction of the Muslim shrines might lead to World War III, say that the decision does not fall under their jurisdiction, but rather that it is one to be decided by *halacha*, or religious law.

Halacha law states clearly that no Jew may enter the holy mount until the coming of the Jewish Messiah. So ruled the noted 12th-century Spanish rabbi-philosopher Maimonides, as well as Israel's first chief rabbi, Avraham Yitzhak Hacohen Kook. Although most Orthodox Jews rigorously adhere to this *halacha* ban, many other Jews—orthodox and secular—do not.

Since 1967—the year the Israelis seized military control of

Jerusalem, Jewish nationalists, many of them armed Israeli rabbis, officers, soldiers and religious students, have on 100 or more occasions stormed the Muslim grounds. Chief Chaplain of the Armed Forces, Shlomo Goren (who later became Israel's chief rabbi) was one of the first to disobey the centuries-old *halacha* ban. In August 1967, he led 50 armed extremists onto the site in order, he claimed, to conduct "a religious service."

In most all armed assaults on Haram al-Sharif, religious Israeli youths have been led by militant rabbis. "We should not forget," said Rabbi Shlomo Chaim Hacohen Aviner "that the supreme purpose of the ingathering of exiles and the establishment of our state is the building of the temple. The temple is the very top of the pyramid."

In the two decades (1967 to 1986) that Jewish militants have made sabotage attempts on the mosque, the chief Sephardic and Ashkenazic rabbis have never condemned the Jewish militants. "The chief rabbis, who even receive their salaries from the state, haven't condemned at all the violence committed. This signals that it is not so terrible," an Israeli journalist noted.

For some years now, Muslim authorities have feared that armed Jewish militants who storm the holy grounds and excavate underneath the mosque are intent on destroying their holy shrines. Speaking at a 1983 press conference, Sheikh Muhammad Shakra, director of Al-Aqsa Mosque, said Israeli archaeological excavations under the mosque had brought to light only relics from the Omayyad Abbassid and Ottoman eras. He added that the Israelis had found no clues that a temple ever stood there.

The most damaging Israeli intrusion on the Supreme Muslim Council authorities has occured, quite literally, under their feet. Since the early 1970s, the Israeli ministry of religious affairs has been digging a tunnel along the edge of the Haram, underneath a number of historic buildings. Its aim is to locate possible clues that the second temple stood on this site. According to Adnan Husseini, who is in charge of Muslim properties, the tunnel now stretches over 1,000 feet (more than the length of three football fields). From an engineering point of view, the tunnel was not dug scientifically. Five buildings, including several schools and offices of the Muslim authorities, now have structural problems. The cracking has occurred gradually as the tunnel proceeds.

In Jerusalem, I interviewed an American archaeologist, Gordon Franz of Fair Lawn, New Jersey, who spent two years on digs while a resident at Jerusalem's Holy Land Institute. Together we visited in West Jerusalem a model of ancient Jerusalem in the era of Christ, or, as the Israelis say, at the time of the Second Temple. As we stood, looking at the model, which is the size of a large living room, I asked: Was there any evidence that the temple was located where the designer put it in this model? That is, on the site where the Dome of Rock and Al-Aqsa stand today?

"There's no evidence either way, that it was there or that it was not there. Some people assume that the temple was there."

Did he mean that Avi-Yonah, the Israeli-Jewish designer of the model, made that assumption?

"Yes. He made the asumption because he and most other Jews want to believe the temple was there.

"There are several theories about the temple: Many say it was located where the Dome of the Rock is today. So Zionists say, 'Well, the mosque has got to go' and they say that an act of God, like an earthquake, will destroy it or somebody is going to put dynamite there.

"Former Ashkenazi Chief Rabbi Goren believes the temple was located slightly north of the Dome of the Rock. A third idea is the temple was located on the northern side of the platform. They suggest that the Holy of Holies is over near the Dome of the Spirit.

"A fourth idea is that the temple is already built—in the form of a great synagogue on George V street, in West Jerusalem. And those holding this theory quote from Isaiah, where the question is asked, Where is my house? They interpret this text to mean the temple was not on the present Muslim grounds, but somewhere else."

Franz said that when he goes with Christians to the holy mount, "I like to remind them that Christ used a geographical location to convey a spiritual truth. As you recall, religious leaders always were reminding Christ that they were holy, as was their father Abraham. To teach them that spirituality did not come from one's lineage or even from worshiping in a temple, Christ told them, 'You are of your father the devil'—that's in John 8:44. Always," Franz added,

"Christ taught that God did not reside in a temple, but in the souls of men and women."

As regards the subject of a temple, "It is is a big controversy." Where did Franz think a temple stood 2,000 years ago?

"I don't know," he said. "No one really knows. But I do know that those who say they want a temple want primarily to destroy the mosque. Now I have no idea how the destruction is going to happen. But it is going to happen. They are going to build a temple there. But how, who, when, where—don't ask me."

One Israeli, Scottish immigrant Asher S. Kaufman, claims he has positive proof that the Jewish temples did not stand on the site of the present Dome of the Rock, but rather south of there. Kaufman, who is not an archaeologist but a Hebrew University physics professor, wrote a lengthy article in the March-April 1983 issue of the *Biblical Archaeology Review* (BAR) in which he stated that his research, paid for by the Israeli Government, "precludes any other interpretation."

For an analysis of the Kaufman article, I talked with an American archaeologist, James E. Jennings, who lives in Chicago and has done extensive archaeological field work in Egypt, Jordan and Palestine, serving as project director, organizer and field archaeologist for five expeditions, one under sponsorship of the Smithsonian Institution.

Does he as an archaeologist and long-term student of Haram al-Sharif agree with the findings of the Israeli physics professor?

"I feel strongly that the study is politically motivated and that sober research could raise innumerable objections to it," Dr. Jennings said. "I object to the sources and what might be 'atmospherics' or the climate in which the work was undertaken.

"I object most seriously to its methodology and the use of biased, compounded assumptions and arbitrariness. I believe that a new study might well produce a different conclusion. This Israeli physicist is interested in tying in the Dome of the Tablets, which marks a holy site, with the temple, and he talks about the threshing floor of the Jebusites mentioned in the story of David in the Old Testament and tries to tie that in. And there are certain cuttings on the rock, which he can measure and establish a distance. Kaufman has an interesting theory, but in general it is somewhat less than 50 percent probable."

What, I asked Jennings, might be Israel's political advantage in supporting and publicizing a study that in effect tells the world: we don't need to destroy the mosque to build our temple? We will put it alongside the Dome of the Rock.

"Many Israeli Zionists like to go step by step. If they do not blow up the mosque, they hope to be seen as moderate. Rather than risk a cataclysmic holy war with the 150 million Muslims who surround Israel, some Israeli leaders seem to be testing the political climate for building a temple alongside the mosque. If they can get by with this, they might later on decide to confiscate all of the Muslim holy grounds of Haram al-Sharif. It's a political power play.

"Don't forget, some of the most fanatic leaders in the plan to destroy the mosque are not religious Jews but militant Zionists. They may not believe in God, but they want a temple for nationalistic, political reasons. And it's not that they want a temple so much as they want to negate the presence of the mosque. As ardent Zionists, they want to eliminate Muslim shrines. They believe that is what any good Zionist should do," Dr. Jennings concluded.

It was in 1979 that I first heard Jewish settlers illegally encamped on Palestinian lands quite openly discuss plans to destroy the Dome of the Rock and Al-Aqsa. While staying in the occupied West Bank with Gush Emunim or Bloc of the Faithful Jewish settlers in their strange ghettos, protected by high barbed wire fences, search beams and armed sentries, I listened as they boasted of breaking laws and creating new "facts."

"If destroying the mosque to build a temple creates a big war, then so be it," the Gush settlers, about one-third of them dual Israeli-American citizens, told me. As "pioneers" with army-issued weapons, they seek excitement, adventure and a new challenge. "In the beginning when we could practice guerrilla-type tactics to seize land and make our settlements it was exciting," Bobby Brown from Brooklyn explained. Shifting his Israeli army-issued submachine gun, he added:

"Now we are getting bored. We are fully armed. And we feel it is a stain on our land to have a mosque sitting in our midst. You look at any picture of Jerusalem and you see that mosque! That will have to go. One day we will build our Third Temple there. We must do this to show the Arabs, and all the world, that we Jews have sovereignty over all of Jerusalem, over all the Land of Israel."

Brown and I were sitting in a prefabricated home in a colony near Bethlehem called Tekoa, built on land Brown admits he and other recent immigrants confiscated by armed force from Palestinians. In that year, 1979, Brown told me that he and other Gush settlers would be deeply involved in politics. "We will have our own party, called Tehiya. We will use members of this party to lobby, to press for a program to build our temple."

To build a temple for prayer was one thing, I suggested. But destroying the mosque could ignite an apocalyptic war between Israel and the Arabs.

"Exactly," said Brown. "But we want that kind of war—because we will win it. We will then expel all of the Arabs from the Land of Israel, we will rebuild our temple and await our Messiah."

In early 1979, a group of ultra-Orthodox Gush Emunim settlers met in an apartment of one of their spiritual leaders in Kiryat Arba, a Jewish colony placed in the heart of the otherwise exclusively Palestinian town of Hebron. They met to discuss sabotaging the Camp David accords. "We feared these accords would lead to an independent Palestinian state," Brown explained. The settlers' spiritual advisors were Rabbi Moshe Levinger and Rabbi Eliazer Waldman, a parliamentary member of the Tehiya party.

Robert I. Friedman in the *Village Voice* (November 12, 1985) writes that in their earliest meeting, Gush members—"composed of army officers and leading right-wing personalities, men with friendships that reached high into the Begin government"—decided to blow up the Dome of the Rock. Names of the Jewish terrorists and details of their acts became known in 1984 after a trial in which most signed confessions of the crimes of which they were accused.

Friedman writes graphically of Gush fanatics who formed "the most violent subversive organization in Israel's history." He gives details on how they plotted to destroy the mosque:

"Menachem Livni, the bearded, stern-faced commander of a reserve battalion of combat engineers in the Israeli army and the leader of the Gush underground, obtained aerial photos of the mosque and recruited an air force pilot to steal a plane and strafe it. But Livni later opted for a ground attack.

"Squads of bomb-laden Jews were to scale the Old City walls into the mosque's courtyard. A model of the mosque was built; practice runs were timed; homemade explosives were tested in the desert. Livni calculated which way the mosque would fall after it exploded and how far the schrapnel would be catapulted. It was imperative not to harm Jews in the neighboring quarter, nor to damage the Western Wall. Finally, the conspirators obtained silencers for the Uzis and tear gas grenades to overcome the mosque's Islamic guards."

At the same time the Gush fanatics were plotting to blow up the mosque, they also plotted to kill three Palestinian mayors—Ibrahim Tawil of El Bireh, Karim Khalif of Ramallah and Bassam Shaka of Nablus—by planting bombs in their cars. Tawil escaped injury but a grenade rigged to his garage blinded an Israeli disposal expert. Khalif lost a foot, and Shaka, the most seriously injured, lost both legs. Reporter Friedman gives us ample evidence that many high placed Israelis looked upon the maiming of the Palestinian mayors with satisfaction:

"Two days after the West Bank bombings, the Jewish Regional Council of Judea and Samaria—a committee of the elected leaders from the Jewish West Bank settlements—held its monthly meeting with Brigadier General Ben Eliazer, commander of the West Bank. According to two settlers who were at the meeting, Eliazer expressed satisfaction with the attacks on the mayors, allegedly saying that he was only sorry that the would-be assassins had done 'half a job.' "

"Everyone around the table was happy," recalled council member Pincus Villershtine of Ofra (an illegal Jewish settlement). "We were all smiling."

Natan Nathanson, head of security at the West Bank Jewish colony called Shilo, who had been part of the team that planted the bomb in Shaka's car, left the meeting, Friedman reported, feeling the underground had the tacit support of the Israeli military and government at the highest level. He interpreted Eliazer's remarks as a signal that the underground had done something for "the glory and security of the people of Israel."

All over the West Bank, "Jewish settlers and soldiers celebrated the attacks on the mayors," said Benzion Heineman, who was sentenced to three years in prison for his role in the Gush underground. "When they heard about Shaka at the military headquarters in Nablus, the military government and soldiers made a *b'raha* (a blessing) over wine," Heineman told reporter Friedman.

Israeli deputy attorney general Yehudit Karp was chosen to head a secret blue-ribbon commission to investigate the allegations. After more than a year of work, the commission submitted its report, which revealed that Israeli police and military officials had acquiesced in vigilante attacks against West Bank Palestinians.

In his *Village Voice* article, Friedman reports that a secret commission, headed by Israeli deputy attorney general Yehudit Karp, was formed to investigate allegations that Jewish extremists were being given free reign: "In 1983 Karp resigned from the commission, charging that Begin was suppressing the report because it was a political liability. Describing law enforcement in the occupied territories as 'lackadaisical' and 'ineffective,' Karp asked, 'How is it possible that they (the Israeli government) take measures against each Arab stone thrower, yet fail to bring to justice (Jewish) settlers who open fire on Arabs?'

"During the trial, attorneys for the Gush terrorists came up with a politically explosive defense: that Shin Bet (Israel's FBI) knew the identities of the Jewish terrorists soon after their attack on the mayors and had prior knowledge of a Jewish attack on an Islamic College. Shin Bet failed to arrest anyone, according to chief defense attorney Avi Yitzahk, because 'top political and military authorities had urged the underground to take actions that a democratic state cannot.'

"The truth about the level of government involvement in the Gush Emunim underground may never be known," reporter Friedman noted.

In July 1985 an Israeli judge sentenced 18 members of the Gush underground to prison terms ranging from four months to life. As he read out his sentences, the judge added that the convicted men should be praised "for their pioneering ethos and war records."

The following day, Friedman reports, Vice Premier Shamir began to press for clemency. Speaking to graduates of the right-wing Betar youth movement in Jerusalem, Shamir said that the members of the underground were "excellent people."

Rabbi Waldman, named by Menachem Livni as having given approval to the West Bank bombings, was another ardent sup-porter of clemency. "They (the members of the underground) are devoted citizens who must be released from prison so that they can continue to build the country . . . It will weaken the government if they are held in jail . . . Clemency is necessary," the rabbi told Friedman.

Throughout the trial the Orthodox Jewish terrorists portrayed themselves as defenders of Jewish rights in the West Bank. Yehuda Etzion, the conspirators' spiritual ideologue, told the court that in 1981 he began to consider the necessity of "purifying" the Muslim site by removing the Islamic shrine, a mission, he be-lieved, that should have been carried out by the state immediately following the 1967 war. When the government did not act, Etzion said in his testimony, he realized that he himself would have to blow up the Muslim shrines since "the state of Israel was not interested in achieving redemption."

In spite of the gravity of the crimes, the Israeli court judges handed down astonishingly light sentences. The judges were forced by law to give mandatory life imprisonment to three defen-dants convicted of murder. But having discretionary power in other instances, they handed down prison terms ranging from three to seven years.

As the judges announced their lenient sentences, the atmo-sphere in the packed courtroom became "a carnival," an Israeli reporter wrote. Spectators hugged and kissed the defendants and some sang Jewish nationalist songs as the convicted settlers con-gratulated one another. Supporters from West Bank settlements proclaimed the defendants "heroes of Israel."

The defendants "should get medals. They were chosen by God to change the Jewish law of this country. The law is in the hands of God," said Shoshana Helkiriyahu, 60, who immigrated from New York in 1935 and lives in the illegal Jewish Kiryet Arba settlement near Hebron.

"I told my son, 'Now you have to do the same as they did so that there will be more people in the Land of Israel who want to get rid of the Arabs,' " Helkiriyahu said.

The Jewish terrorists, while not a political force in themselves, have become the fulcrum of Israeli fascism. Though at the time of their arrest, only the Tehiya party and Kahane's Kach movement openly came out in their defense, by July 1985 all the right-wing and clerical parties as well as some Labor party members were working for their release. Parliament members Ariel Sharon and Geula Cohen, as well as other high ranking Israelis called the convicted criminals "great heroes."

Of his light sentence and possible future pardon, Etzion, 34, said he knew the trial would take place but he added, "I think that in the court of history I'm 100 percent not guilty because the building (Dome of the Rock) will be removed."

In raising money for the Jewish terrorists, *Jewish Press* editor Yehuda Schwartz told Robert Friedman in the forementioned *Village Voice* article that he worked closely with Rabbi Avi Weiss, head of the Hebrew Institute in Riverdale, New York. Weiss said he separately collected about $100,000 from American Jews to defray the terrorists' legal expenses. Charlie Fox, an elderly Jew in Florida, contributed $75,000 of that sum.

"Neither Schwartz nor Weiss has registered—or filed financial statements—with the New York State Attorney General's office, or with the Secretary of State's office," wrote Friedman. State law "requires any non-profit charity raising in excess of $10,000 a year to register with the Secretary of State's office. Charities must also register with the State Attorney General's office. Additional sums of money have been collected for the Gush underground in right-wing Orthodox synagogues across America." Friedman added that Rabbi Maurice Lamm of the Beth Jacob Congregation in Beverly Hills, California, raised "very large sums of money" for the terrorists. Rabbi Lamm, who made appeals for donations from his pulpit, said he sent the money to Rabbi Moshe Levinger, spiritual leader of Gush Emunim, in occupied Hebron.

Friedman reports that "over the years, the Gush Emunim

settlers movement also has reaped a harvest in America, where it has collected hundreds of thousands of dollars in private donations, according to Israeli reporter Danny Rubinstein, *Davar's* West Bank correspondent and author of a book on Gush Emunim. The movement's largest contributor, Rubinstein says, has been Marcus Katz, a wealthy arms dealer of Mexican nationality, who represented the Israeli arms industry in Iran and later in Central America. Katz also helped finance a legal battle waged by Ariel Sharon against *Time* magazine. Cyril Stein, known as the king of London's gambling industry, also has given substantial sums to Gush Emunim, according to Rubinstein."

The U.S. Treasury provides the largest source of funding for the Gush Emunim and their illegal West Bank settlements. Hundreds of millions of taxpayers' dollars have been funneled into building the illegal Jewish settlements and their costly infrastructure. For example, Rubinstein told Friedman, many Gush terrorists were also employed by the Israeli government as West Bank functionaries.

Despite the conviction of the Gush terrorists, Friedman reports that the movement itself remains committed to its messianic mission: "Their notion of a Zionist order is a dark mixture of religious fanaticism and brutal chauvinism which takes precedence over the laws of the state," wrote S. Zalman Abramov, a former Likud deputy speaker of the Israeli parliament. "Maybe some of the terrorists will regret their actions after the shock of what they have been through. This is not what will happen, however, to the Gush itself. They will continue to cling to their faith and their path, assured of the admiration of many government leaders. The hothouse which nurtured the scourge of terror is alive and well and shows absolutely no sign of regret."

Research done by Robert Friedman indicates that Meir Kahane, the rabble-rousing rabbi from Brooklyn, has been even more successful than the Gush in tapping American Jewish support. Since founding the Jewish Defense League (JDL) in 1968, Kahane has collected millions of dollars from American Jewish businessmen. Among the wealthy Jews who have supported the JDL is Reuben Mattus, the founder and president of Haagen-Dazs ice cream. "If they needed money, I gave it," Mattus told

Friedman.

According to Friedman, Rabbi Kahane says that donations to him have increased "especially from Jewish millionaires," since his election to the Knesset. Currently, his largest bastions of support are in New York and Los Angeles. "He has received substantial sums from extremely prominent businessmen, well-known in the Jewish community," Rabbi Jack Simcha Cohen of Temple Shaarei Tefila of Los Angeles, who himself has collected money on behalf of the Gush underground, told Friedman.

"The emotional and financial level of support for Kahane in my district is tremendous," Assemblyman Hikind, whose district has the largest Jewish constituency in New York State, told Friedman. "After Kahane won a Knesset seat, many people from my district came to me emotionally high from his victory. Kahane is one of the great men in the Jewish community today!"

According to Friedman, in May 1984 Kahane traveled to Dallas with Jimmy DeYoung, a born again Christian vice president and general manager of religious radio station WNYM in New York. The two appeared on a television talk show. Later Kahane attended private cocktail parties where he reportedly solicited funds from Christian evangelicals.

Kahane, who writes a weekly column for the *Jewish Press*, where he was once an editor, has used the paper to solicit funds for Kach members convicted of terrorist activities, Friedman reports. The JDL, however, is still one of Kahane's most lucrative sources of funding for his activities in Israel, although he stepped down as head of the organization in August 1984. The JDL is listed with the New York Secretary of State's office as having a religious exemption from filing financial statements—"a neat trick for a group that is listed as a terrorist organization by the FBI," reporter Friedman noted.

In October 1985 the State Department stripped Kahane of his U.S. citizenship. He continued to shuttle, however, with ease between Israel and the United States.

Friedman writes: "In pursuit of his messianic vision, Kahane has sought alliances not only with American Jews but also with right-wing Christian evangelists in America, who, like him, believe that Jews are God's Chosen People and that the Messiah's coming is linked to the Jewish return to Israel and the expulsion of Israel's enemies—the Arabs."

Since my research leads me to believe that the Middle East, which is receiving more weapons than any other area of the world, represents the most dangerous powder keg for a nuclear conflagration, I still could not comprehend why Christians such as Reisenhoover, DeLoach, Hilton Sutton, Douglas Krieger, Charles Monroe—none of whom look anything at all like fanatics who would go on a suicidal mission—had banded together to aid Jewish terrorists destroy Muslim shrines. Nor could I understand why one member of that group, Pastor DeLoach, would claim if they started World War III, they were doing God's will.

For additional perspective on such thinking, I arranged an interview with Professor Gordon Welty of Wright State University in Ohio. A sociologist and anthropologist, he has traveled throughout the Middle East and has written and lectured extensively on the subject of the Christian right-wing support for Israel. Our schedules were such that both of us were to be in Chicago, and we met there in a hotel restaurant and talked over lunch.

How, I asked, can Christians consider it moral to negate the existence of about a billion Muslims and praiseworthy to donate millions of dollars for the destruction of their holy shrine?

"The evangelical-fundamentalists who raise money to destroy the mosque practice the same type of muscular theology that many of our forefathers did. They thought it brave, moral and right 'to win the West,' to slaughter Indians and march forward with white civilization. Since the 'frontier' of America is gone, they seek to recreate it elsewhere. The 'New Zion' of the settler's dreams has become the plain old Zion of Palestine.

"Just as some Christian settlers found it moral to kill Indians, some Christians now find it moral to give money to Zionists who kill Palestinians," Dr. Welty said. "With a disdain of history and sociological laws, they make invisible those who stand in the path of their manifest destiny. Now that the West is won, the Reisenhoovers must fly over to Israel.

"One of the best descriptions I've seen of this type of power-makes-right is given by John Hobson in his book, *Imperialism*. He calls it 'muscular Christianity.' It translates into a rough-

and-ready, take-what-you-can brand of action. The 'muscular Christians' supporting Zionism settle for short-term goals and deal in strange inconsistencies. They compartmentalize: they hold in one section of their brains the conviction that the Jews are God's Chosen People, and in another compartment they believe God does not hear the prayers of the Jew. They have, to a marked degree, this ability to hold incompatible and often self-contradictory ideas and motives.

"Thus, they do not 'see' Palestinians, they do not 'see' the mosque—they only say 'they must go.' "

What, I asked, about Pastor DeLoach's fascination with the reinstitution of animal sacrifice to please God? He proudly said he hosted in his Houston home two Israeli religious students who were studying how to kill sheep in a temple service.

"Yes, can't you imagine bonfires, the bleating of lambs being slaughtered—the blood, the smell of burning flesh, all to please God! Both the Jews and the Christians who want this are ignoring or abandoning the most valuable theological and moral precepts of the Hebrew prophetic tradition. What Yahweh really demanded was not the blood of sheep and goats but, in the words of Amos, justice and righteousness."

The main reason, I recalled to Professor Welty, that Pastor DeLoach gave for favoring the removal of a Muslim shrine for the building of a Jewish temple was that, as he put it, Christians must have "freedom" to worship on that particular holy site in Jerusalem.

"Yes, freedom is one of the 'masked words' the muscular Christians like most to use. Yet, does Pastor DeLoach think for a moment he would have the 'freedom' to preach a sermon anywhere in the Jewish state? Does he think he would have the 'freedom' to speak about Christ to any Israeli Jew? Does he think he would have the 'freedom' as a Christian to immigrate to the Jewish state? Since citizenship is reserved only for Jews, he would not have that freedom."

Since Pastor DeLoach had said he was concerned only about a Christian's freedom to pray at Haram al-Sharif, was the pastor, I asked, being hypocritical?

"No, not in the least," Professor Welty said. "If the minister is typical of the muscular Christians I have studied, he is incapable of being hypocritical. Their power is to keep inconsistencies in air-tight compartments, so that they themselves never recognize these inconsistencies. As far as the muscular Christians know (or accept) they act with high minded, upright, self-sacrificing, generous, moral rectitude." In this context, Dr. Welty concluded, if the money a muscular Christian donates to the Jewish terrorists buys the dynamite that destroys the mosque, the muscular Christian will say, simply:

"It was an act of God."

Soon after this interview, I read an Israeli public opinion poll published in 1984 showing that 18.7 percent of the Israeli public support terrorist activities by extremist Jewish groups. In commenting on the poll, the Israeli writer Yehoehus Sobol pointed out that in 1938, a representative sample of the Nazi Party members found that 63 percent of them objected to hurting Jews, 32 percent expressed apathy on the subject and only five percent were in favor of harming Jews.

Four years later, in 1942, when the annihilation of Jews was already speedily taking place, a representative sampling of the Nazi Party members showed that those against attacking Jews decreased to 26 percent, while the number of apathetic increased to 69 percent. The number of Nazis in favor of attacking Jews remained the same: five percent.

"It is clear," Sobol said, "that during the activation of the policy of genocide toward the Jewish people, only five percent of the Nazi Party members were prepared to identify with the policy . . . Now after 50 years, there is no justification anymore for ignoring a danger that is embodied in a fragmented-fanatic minority. A careful examination of the distribution of the views and positions in German society in the Nazi period has left no excuse for anyone today to claim that as long as racist ideas belong only to a small minority, there is no basis on which to speak about the fascistization of the whole society.

"The opposite is true: the German experience proves that fascistization of the society begins where racist ideas and extreme chauvinism belong to a small minority on the extreme right whose activities are carried out against the background of the majority's apathy."

Fanatics who belong to what the vast majority of Christians and Jews might term a crazy minority—and numbering no more than five percent of the total Israeli population—are nevertheless capable of destroying Islam's most holy shrine in Jerusalem, an act that could easily trigger a worldwide war involving Russia and the United States. The only necessary condition for this to happen is the existence of a decisive majority of the apathetic. The main-line Israeli and American Jews, together with non-Zionist American Christians, may well represent the decisive apathetic majority.

This decisive apathetic majority provides breeding grounds for the religious extremists. Increasingly, terrorists are recognized as heroes and, if sentenced, do not serve their full terms in jail. On December 8, 1985, President Chaim Herzog of Israel commuted the prison sentences of two Jewish terrorists who had been convicted of plotting to blow up Jerusalem's most holy Islamic shrine.

The prisoners freed are Dan Beeri, 41, and Yosef Tzuria, 26, who were serving three-year terms for plotting to blow up the Dome of the Rock and Al-Aqsa Mosque. According to court records, the terrorists' plan was to dynamite and destroy the shrine to provoke the Islamic world into a holy war with Israel.

They are now free to continue the plot.

No Christian to Guide Us

On both Falwell-sponsored tours, when I disembarked an El Al non-stop 747 New York to Tel Aviv flight, I was one more tourist with dollars to bolster the Israeli economy—dollars that even on a package tour would be distributed to a wide variety of Israelis throughout the economy: Israelis who run hotels and restaurants, own and operate taxicabs, bus lines, tourist agencies and souvenir shops, as well as Israelis who stamp passports, and move baggage and own and operate tourist agencies and act as guides.

On the 1983 tour I was one of 630 pilgrims who each paid more than $1,000, which represents a total sum of more than $630,000. On the 1985 tour, I was one of 850 pilgrims who paid about $1,300, or a total sum, a Jerusalem tour operator told me, that translates into more than a million dollars for Falwell and the state of Israel. With this group, one among literally hundreds of similar package tours, "Falwell probably made a quarter of a million dollars—and Israel three-quarters of a million," the tour operator said.

Since its creation in 1948, Israel increasingly has benefited from tourism. In one decade (1967–1977) after prop planes were replaced by jets, international tourism increased nearly 75 percent, producing 243 million international tourists in 1977. Between 1970 and 1975, international tourist receipts more than doubled, from $18.2 billion to $38.8 billion.

By the 1970s, international tourism operations brought in almost as much revenue as the overall value of the world production of aluminum, lead, copper and iron ore combined. And despite recession, unemployment, oil crisis, inflation and political upheaval, tourism unabatedly continued its upward spiral. By the mid-1980s, tourism was bringing in more money than oil and employing more people than any other activity. It held the number one position among all industries.

As many as 100,000 tourists visit Jerusalem each year, and since each foreign visitor leaves more than $700 in Israel, they represent about a billion-dollar-a-year industry for the Israelis. Tourists account for about six percent of the Gross National Product and represent an important foreign exchange earner for the beleagured Israeli economy.

For over a thousand years, Christians, Muslims and Jews have gone as tourists to Jerusalem. However, since 1967 when Israelis gained military control of Jerusalem, only Christian and Jewish tourists go there in large numbers. While nearly a billion Muslims over the world revere Jerusalem as one of their most sacred shrines and presumably would want to travel there, most of them cannot at present do so since the Arab states have never, with the exception of Egypt, recognized that Israel is a bona fide entity. (Indonesians, citizens of the world's largest Muslim country, can get to Jerusalem but in the main are not interested as long as Jerusalem is militarily occupied by Israeli soldiers.)

Israel can attract only a limited number of Jewish tourists. Worldwide, Jews number only 14 million, and of this total well over three million are Israeli citizens. To increase tourist dollars, Israelis must look to the Christians, who number one billion worldwide and account for more than 70 percent of Israel's tourism revenue. Conservative Christians, including evangelicals, fundamentalists, Pentecostals and charismatics, supply most of that revenue.

When Prime Minister Begin came into office, he personally met with evangelical-fundamentalists to help plan package tours. In early 1981 Begin chose the intimacy of his home to entertain an Assemblies of God evangelist, Reverend David Lewis, and his wife. He discussed tourist package plans with the Springfield, Missouri, minister, who that year created Lewis Tours to move thousands of evangelicals to Israel.

Tourist dollars also helped cement the close relationship between Israeli leaders and Falwell. In 1982, Falwell dispatched Ronald Godwin and 37 other Moral Majority organizers for a week's stay in Israel, where they collaborated with top Israelis devising package plans for Christian pilgrims. They agreed on arrangements that were relatively simple, with each partner gaining monetarily.

Falwell would collect names and money. He would instruct pilgrims to make their way individually to New York's JFK airport, where the Israelis would take charge. They would book all pilgrims on the Israeli El Al airlines and once the Christians were on Israeli soil, Israeli guides with Israeli ground transport companies would shepherd the Christians about. As for the proceeds, Falwell's Moral Majority would get a slice of the pie, with the bigger chunk going to Israel.

Israel also benefits economically from the International Christian Embassy, created in 1980. In that year, Prime Minister Begin illegally annexed Arab East Jerusalem. And in protest 13 foreign embassies moved their offices from West Jerusalem to Tel Aviv. To offset disapproval by the secular powers, the Israelis encouraged evangelical-charismatics to form an "embassy" to express approval. In opening ceremonies attended by leading Israeli officials, 1,000 Christians, representing 23 nations, stepped forward to pledge their support.

It was widely alleged, and brought out in a court hearing, that New Zealand, Austrian, Dutch and American money poured into this embassy and was passed on to militant Israeli groups to aid in the expulsion of Palestinians and the removal of Muslim shrines in the Old City, to prepare grounds for the building of a Jewish temple. Money was also provided to set up programs to bring in large numbers of Christian tourists to Israel.

The embassy chose a major Jewish day, the Feast of the Tabernacles, or Succoth, and built a tourist promotional package around that special day. Working with Israel's tourism department, the embassy devised a ten-day program for Christians that includes El Al air fare, room, meals and sightseeing. The embassy sells this plan almost exclusively to evangelical-charismatics, who cherish a belief system that God's countdown on history has begun, with all major events to take place in Israel. In 1982 the Christian Embassy brought over 2,000 pilgrims, in 1983 about 3,000 and by 1985, it sponsored more than 5,000 U.S. Christians, the vast majority American charismatics.

The charismatics, more openly demonstrative of their faith than most Christian sects, shout, sing and dance through Jerusalem streets for a week and turn the Feast of the Tabernacles into a kind of Mardi Gras. In 1982, Prime Minister Begin, overlooking the carnival atmosphere, warmly welcomed the charismatics, proclaiming they provide "great satisfaction." Presumably, part of the satisfaction came with the three and a half million tourist dollars they left in Israeli hands. The celebration in 1985 earned, according to Timothy King, financial officer for the Christian Embassy, "between 15 and 20 million" tourist dollars, most of it going to Israel.

By 1985, many Israeli leaders recommended the country make greater efforts to attract Christian tourists. Tourism Minister Avraham Sharir told a cabinet session devoted to tourism that for every dollar the government invested in tourism, the country reaped $150 in return. He suggested they spend even more than the current $3 million annually earmarked for promotion and advertising. Tourism, he said, was Israel's leading product.

On each Falwell tour, we listened to generals and politicians and visited Israeli farms, battlefields and shrines to the dead. Travelers to foreign countries often visit farms, battlefields and shrines to the dead, and may even hear local military chiefs and politicians. The Falwell fare seemed unusual only because we were in the Holy Land, and most travelers traditionally have gone there for a spiritual renewal and not to immerse themselves, as we did, almost entirely in learning about the country's present-day politics.

"Yours is not a 'regular' tour group," David Frank, Jerusalem whole tour operator who handled the Falwell delegation, wrote me. "You are visiting the Holy Land with one of the greatest friends the modern/ancient State of Israel has ever had—Reverend Jerry Falwell. Jerry's friendship for the people of Israel is as pure as his love of the United States . . . By associating with Jerry Falwell, Dr. Ron Godwin and the Moral Majority—and their great support of Israel—you too are a great friend of ours."

All groups traveling to Israel are required by Israeli law to have an Israeli guide, licensed by the Israeli Government Tourist Office. However, if Falwell had so desired, he could have contested this ruling, since by international protocol pilgrim groups are not regarded as tourists and may be guided by pilgrims. Falwell apparently does not wish to categorize himself as a pilgrim.

Rather, as a promoter of Friendship Tours to Israel, Falwell is able to meet top Israeli leaders. On several occasions he met with the Likud leader Begin when he was prime minister and in 1985 he met with the Labor leader Peres, who was then prime minister.

On each tour, Falwell gave the impression he was more interested in selling us on the idea that Israel needs more U.S. weapons—today it has more tanks than France and Germany and the third largest air force in the world—than he was in promoting reconciliation and peace.

On each tour, I attempted to count the hours we spent at Christian sites and hearing about Christ, and the time we spent learning the political and military achievements of the Zionist state. I came up with a ratio of about one to 30. That is, for every hour for Christ's teachings, we spent about 30 hours on the political-military aspects of Israeli life. We heard the words of Jesus read from the New Testament on three occasions: one being at Caesarea—a Christian lay leader read Acts 24:1–9; the second time at the site where Jesus said to Peter, "Upon this rock I will build my church," and the third time on the Sea of Galilee.

Why would Christian ministers such as Falwell, Hilton Sutton of Texas, or Chuck Smith of California, take Christians to the Land of Christ and choose not to guide them to the sites where Christ was born, had his ministry and died? I think of three reasons: first some ministers might make the tours for the money involved. Second, some ministers, like the rest of us, might be susceptible to flattery. Most of the American Christian ministers who take an initial tour to the Holy Land are viewed by the Israelis as potential tour leaders for groups of Christians. The Israelis offer them flattering travel grants, red-carpet hospitality and reduced rates or free tickets on El Al. Most of the ministers going to Israel have never personally met leaders of a nation. The Israelis make time for them and talk over war strategy. The Israelis provide helicopters and guides to give the ministers conducted tours of the Golan Heights and they repeatedly tell the ministers that Israel is the only friend America has in the Middle East.

The Israelis gave that kind of attention to the Reverend Bailey Smith of Oklahoma, after he told a meeting sponsored by the Religious Roundtable of Dallas that "God Almighty does not hear the prayer of a Jew." Rather than rebuke him, the Israelis invited him to visit Israel, with the Israelis picking up the tab for all expenses. Smith accepted, and at the conclusion of his visit he promised: "The bottom line is that you're going to read my name many times in the future in activities supporting the Jewish people and Israel." He then inaugurated a series of joint Baptist-Jewish programs and economic ties.

How many Christian pastors, I asked a prominent Presbyterian minister, did he estimate went on subsidized trips to the Holy Land?

"In recent years, of those I know who have traveled there, I would say 90 percent have had their trips partially or wholly paid for by Israeli or Zionist grants, discounts or tie-ins."

Eliot H. Sharp of Brooklyn, New York, who is in his 80s and has long studied the Middle East, told me that he had a relative, a minister, who returned from the Holy Land "strongly biased in favor of Israel." Eliot asked if the Israelis paid his expenses.

"Yes, for the most part," the relative said. "I was one in a group of invited clergy and spouses who had never been to Israel before. While there, the Israelis encouraged us to get other Christians to visit Israel and they indicated they had offered us a subsidized rate based on the expectation that our visit would help increase the number of other tourists."

In concluding the story, Eliot Sharp said he understood that "Every Bible-loving Christian longs, as a Gospel hymn puts it, to 'walk today where Jesus walked.' But if they accept a partially or wholly subsidized trip, they should know the Israelis will want them to leave the land of Christians, Muslims and Jews as my relative did—strongly biased in favor of only one group, the Israelis."

In addition to the possible motives of money and flattery, there's a third and overwhelming reason why Christian ministers go to the Land of Christ and do not speak of Christ and do not choose to see indigenous Christians: They negate or downplay

their allegiance to the Sermon on the Mount in order to upgrade
and strengthen their belief in and their cult worship for the land
of Israel. As one woman on the Falwell tour put it to me, "Jesus
can't return unless there's an Israel for him to return to."

The Reverend Chuck Smith of the Calvary Chapel in Santa
Ana, California, has sponsored more than 2,500 Christians from
Calvary Chapel on journeys to the Holy Land. His members also
have given more than $700,000 for Israel's hospitals—including
an ambulance and emergency relief supplies—and irrigation proj-
ects. In return, the Israelis gave the Reverend Smith permission
to streamline the process of getting baptized in the Jordan, the
site where John the Baptist is said to have immersed Jesus to mark
His coming to divine power and ministry.

Smith, by means that are not clear, seems to have purchased
with donations from his 25,000-member congregation a portion
of the river. He installed chains alongside one side of the river
indicating where Christians by the dozens may enter systemati-
cally, get baptized by immersion and hurriedly exit—much as
one moves in and out of chained corridors in a crowded bank,
post office or supermarket.

In forming their alliance with Falwell and other Christian
Right ministers, the Israelis have insisted that Christian tourists
fly only Israeli El Al airlines, which at one point had complained
of losing traffic to the Royal Jordanian Airlines Alia and had
declared bankruptcy. Previously, many tourists flew Alia into
Amman, Jordan. After two or three days in Jordan, they would
proceed by bus or taxi and at the Allenby Bridge cross the Jordan
river, enter occupied Palestine (the West Bank) and travel a short
distance on to Jerusalem. After spending time in Jerusalem, Bethlehem, Jericho and other sites, the tourists returned to Amman
for a departure flight. About 60,000 persons a year, or roughly six
percent of the total number of Holy Land tourists, did it that way.

In 1981 Prime Minister Begin issued an order to close the
Allenby Bridge to two-way crossings. This order has since been
rescinded, but it established a pattern among many travel agencies
to book Holy Land tourists only on El Al.

Although El Al had urged Begin for economic reasons to
encourage travel exclusively on El Al, Begin took the action "not

so much out of economic considerations for El Al as for political reasons," an Arab Christian travel agent in Jerusalem told me. "Begin wanted only Israeli Jews—not Arab Christians or Arab Muslims—to represent the Holy Land. As long as tourists could book a tour to Jerusalem through Jordanian-based agencies, Begin feared Arabs would exploit these opportunities, that is, tell the tourists our side of the Palestinian-Israeli conflict."

The travel agent's theory was substantiated in an Israeli release quoted in the *New York Times* on July 10, 1981. As far as permitting Palestinians to become guides for visiting tourists, the statement said, "Israeli authorities are known to resent the pro-Arab views they believe are conveyed to the tourists."

"As much as we suffered economically by Begin's stopping two-way traffic from Amman, all of us (Arab tourist operators) are agreed he did this not because we took business from Israeli tourist agencies, but because the Israelis wanted tourists to meet only Israeli Jews—and have no contact with any of us," the Arab Christian said.

In that same year, 1981, the Israeli Ministry of Tourism began applying a regulation requiring that all tourist groups be accompanied by a guide with an Israeli Department of Tourism license. Israeli bus companies stopped renting vehicles to Christian tourists who traveled without an Israeli-licensed guide. And Palestinian priests accompanying pilgrims on religious tours reported they were harassed and intimidated by Israeli police because they did not carry an Israeli license. (In this respect, the Israelis were disregarding international protocol which establishes that pilgrim groups may be guided by pilgrims.)

"Why do I have to hire a guide if I accompany a visiting group of Christians who want to pray in the Holy Sepulcher on Sunday?" Brother Lowenstein of the U.S. Catholic Mission in Jerusalem asked. "The Israelis demand this—for economic and to a greater extent for political reasons. In this manner they control what the tourists see. They generally want them to see only stone monuments and historic sights and to speak only to Israelis.

"The Israeli guide gives them a map of Israel that includes the West Bank and Gaza as part of Israel. In fact, the Israelis have made it illegal to print a map in Israel showing any part as occupied

Palestine. Should anyone ask about Palestine, the Zionist guide will say, 'There is no Palestine.' And should anyone ask about the Palestinians, the guide will say, 'They are all terrorists.' Thus, concluded Brother Lowenstein, "they are successful in giving 95 percent of the Americans only one side of the reality of the Holy Land."

"The so-called non-political trip is impossible," observed Richard Butler, former spokesman for the National Council of Churches of Christ in the United States. "It is in fact very political by what people don't see. To ignore the people of the area and their problems, concerns and hopes is not spiritual." Butler expressed the hope that American Christians visiting the Holy Land would begin to get in touch with area churches, with various viewpoints, and not, as most Christian tourists presently do, limit their contacts to only one group of people and only one viewpoint.

Native Palestinian Christians repeatedly have denounced Israeli regulations that result in visiting pilgrims not being permitted the opportunity of being escorted by Christian guides to the Church of the Nativity in Bethlehem, to the Holy Sepulcher or to the Garden Tomb in Jerusalem.

In March 1984, the Christian Pilgrimage Commission in the Holy Land criticized the Israeli government for restrictions placed on local religious tours. "The Israelis by insisting that all groups have an Israeli guide are violating the freedom of pilgrimage that Christians have enjoyed for 2,000 years," a spokesman for the Christian Commission charged, adding, "Never before has any government tried to control the freedom of pilgrimage to the Holy Land."

Despite the criticism, however, the Israelis continue to insist that all groups be accompanied by a guide bearing an Israeli license. It is generally assumed that the guide with the license will be an Israeli, not an Arab. Since 1967 the Israelis have issued only two official guide licenses to Arabs.

During my 1979 stay in Jerusalem, I asked one Palestinian Christian named Sami, who I knew had applied for the Israeli Ministry of Tourism's licensing course in tour guiding: What happened when he took the examination?

"They gave me verbal and written 'psychotechnic' tests to

examine my knowledge in academic, historical and scientific subjects. They also tested my ability to organize and talk with tourists. I passed my verbal test and my language test"—he speaks English, French, Hebrew, as well as Arabic—"but then they told me I had failed the written exam. I asked to see my test results, but they would not permit this."

And how did he feel about that?

"I am convinced they deliberately denied me the right to study tour guiding because they have a hidden policy to prevent Palestinians from entering the profession. You know," Sami added, "former Israeli Defense Minister Moshe Dayan reportedly once said 'It is easier for Arabs to become Israeli air force pilots than to become tourist guides.' "

If such a hidden policy against Arab guides does exist, were the Israelis discriminating against Palestinians because of economic or political reasons?

"Foremost for political reasons," Sami said. "They worry a great deal about 'image'. They fear that a Palestinian guide might relate incidents that would neutralize or even tarnish their position. The Palestinian guides who were licensed prior to 1967—before the Israelis imposed harsh restrictions—live in fear of saying something the Israelis will interpret as 'political'.

"As an example, a friend who works with the Terra Sancta Travel Agency was speaking to a group of Christians. In answer to a tourist's question about where he was born, he gave the reply, 'in Palestine.' And apparently some Israeli overhearing this answer deemed it too 'political'. And the Israelis revoked his license for six months. So, if you are a Palestinian guide you must try to satisfy a tourist's natural curiosity while steering clear of the Israeli government's obsession with their image."

A Jerusalem *Post* story (February 3, 1985) substantiated much of what Sami had told me. It said only two Palestinian guides have qualified since 1967. And that those who qualified before 1967 retain their licences because of international law regarding military occupation. Most are afraid to speak out regarding the plight of the Palestinians, the story said, and one guide who did in early 1985 was suspended for three months because, according to the Israeli Ministry of Tourism, "he showed a lack of knowledge of the history of the Jewish people in the land of Israel and slandered the state."

Dr. Glen Bowman, a social anthropologist at Oxford University who is writing a book about Christian pilgrimages to the Holy Land, also substantiated what Sami told me. "The Israelis do not want Christians to act as tour guides," he said. "Older guides who have been allowed because of international laws governing occupied territories to retain the licenses are timorous and frightened to talk of the situation of the Palestinian communities." Moreover, said Dr. Bowman, Israeli guides give "reiterated warnings" to Christian tourists that they should not deal with Palestinian shopkeepers. "This sunders one of the few remaining channels of communication between local and visiting populations."

Dr. Bowman says American Christians' negation of Palestinian Christians will inexorably lead us to these developments: First, by urging Israel to fight more wars and take more territories from Arabs, American Christians push Muslim Arabs toward a more strict, militant fundamentalism. By not supplying a lifeline of support for Palestinian Christians, we leave them vulnerable to the most extreme Islamic movement, which, in taking revenge against the West, may turn also on native Christians, seeing them as an appendage to their oppressors. Secondly, if the Palestinian Christian presence continues to be destroyed, the Christian churches will have no presence and no role to play in the Holy Land.

Finally, a militant, nationalist version of Christianity, if not challenged, will replace the primary Christian values of compassion, love and understanding. Then, he warns, Christians will have only a God of war. "Palestinian Christians, largely unperceived by the rest of the Christian world, may prove to be the testing ground of the international Christian community," Dr. Bowman believes. The Palestinians' fate "will determine what role, if any, the foreign churches will play in the future of the Holy Land. And, perhaps in their own communities as well."

Increasingly Palestinian Christians feel themselves in an untenable position. They know that many Muslims, hearing a great deal about Falwell and Robertson, view these dispensationalists as representative of Christianity today. Robertson's "Voice of

Hope" TV station in south Lebanon beams anti-Arab, anti-Muslim messages and supports Israeli take-over of Arab lands. One Palestinian Christian told me: "Muslims, listening to these anti-Arab 'Christian' messages ask, 'How can *you* be Christian?' "

Cirres Elias Nestas told me he and his ancestors, for as long as memory served, were born and grew up in Bethlehem, "when it was a Christian town." When he was a youth, "Bethlehem was 90 percent Christian. Now it is less than 20 percent Christian. This began to happen with the creation of Israel. The Jews wanted an all-Jewish state, with Judaism as the official religion. Now the Christians are moving out of Bethlehem, Nazareth, Jerusalem— from all over the West Bank and Gaza as well as from Israel.

"The Jews encourage this exodus. Many Jews say their aim is to rid Palestine of all the Palestinians, the Christians as well as the Muslims. The Christians we know who are leaving are educated and do not want to work and live under Jewish domination. There is little for them to do here. We cannot lead our own lives here." Nestas estimated that about one hundred thousand Christians have moved out since the Jewish occupation in 1967 of the West Bank.

Figures showing the exodus of Christians from Jerusalem are revealing: in 1940, there were 45,000 Christians living there. By 1960, the number had dropped to 25,000. By 1985, only 10,000 Christians were in Jerusalem.

By early 1986, only 120,000 Christians remained in the area of mandated Palestine (now Israel and the occupied territories).

At the time the British held its mandate over Palestine, Christians represented 15 percent of the population. By early 1986, this had dropped to about eight percent.

Every Christian I met repeatedly said, "If this exodus continues, there will be no Christians left in the land of Christ."

EXPLORING
NON-JEWISH ZIONISM

In late August 1985, I flew from Washington, D. C., to Switzerland to attend the first Christian Zionist Congress held in Basel. I was one of 589 persons from 27 countries attending the Congress, sponsored by the International Christian Embassy of Jerusalem. I went to the Congress hoping to get a definition and a background of political Zionism.

Professor Marvin R. Wilson of Gordon College, Massachusetts, one of the speakers, pointed out that among Jews, there are several definitions and interpretations of Jewish Zionism.

There were in the past, and are today, deeply religious Jews who refer to themselves as Zionists, and there were in the past and are today secular Zionists—Jews who do not believe in God. Theodor Herzl, an Austrian journalist who in 1897 called the first Jewish Zionist Congress in the same Basel musical auditorium where the Christian Zionists met in 1985—was a secular Jew, as was David Ben-Gurion, the first Israeli prime minister. The majority of Israeli Jews today say they do not believe in God—rather they define themselves as secular Jews. *Newsweek* (November 30, 1985) reported that 54 percent of Israelis consider themselves secular Zionists. Other sources put this figure as high as 60-65 percent.

At the first Zionist Congress, Herzl, known as the father of political Jewish Zionism, made an appeal for Jews to live exclusively among Jews. He said all the world hated Jews. And that they could only be safe among themselves.

Eighty-eight years later, in Basel, facing a large portrait of Herzl, I listened to Christian and Israeli Jewish speakers repeat as a litany Herlz's credo: all the world hates Jews. All through history people have hated Jews. There's only one solution: the Jews have to live exclusively among Jews and be militarily strong.

Each speaker emphasized the central conviction of political Zionism: all Gentiles suffer a disease called anti-Semitism (more accurately, anti-Jewishness) and it is an incurable disease. Period. We must recognize this as immutable law, Herzl said. It had no beginning, ending or explanation. It simply was; it existed. It exists.

I listened to the long history of Christian persecution of Jews: Christians expelled Jews from England in the 13th century, from France in the 14th century and from Spain and its possessions, including Sardinia, Sicily and Naples, in 1492. But were the Jews ever the only victims in their times of suffering? In 1492 Ferdinand and Isabella expelled the Muslim Moors. The Jewish minority went with them and, for the most part, settled in Muslim countries. The Spanish royalty then tortured to death those Christians who disagreed with them and sent conquistadores into the Western Hemisphere to rob, subjugate and kill its natives. They gave them only two alternatives, convert or die.

I listened to Christian speakers review the horrors of the holocaust—the Nazi persecution of Jews that provoked worldwide sympathy and led to the creation of a Jewish state. No speaker, Israeli Jew or Christian, however, suggested that somehow we all— all humankind—must in a nuclear age learn to live as good neighbors. Rather than provide hope by suggesting steps whereby Arabs and Jews and all enemies might reach reconciliation and peace, each speaker seemed to reinforce the Jews' haunting fears about security. Rather than stressing how much in common Arabs and Jews have—and indeed how much in common all human beings have—many speakers told us: Jews are different. They must live in an enclave unto themselves.

After three days of listening to political talks, the delegates passed a series of resolutions, which had been written in advance by van der Hoeven of Holland, fervent spokesman for the International Christian Embassy; Johann Luckhoff, a South African who is the Christian Embassy director; Dr. George Giacumakis, former director of the Institute of Holy Land Studies in Jerusalem; Richard Hellman, Christian Embassy representative in Washington, D.C., and others.

In one resolution, the Christian Zionists urged all Jews living outside of Israel to leave the countries where they now are residing and move to the Jewish state. In this resolution, the Christians stated that they realized "the terrible suffering the Jews have experienced" and that since the Jews still face "hateful and destructive forces" they should all—all Jews in America and in every other country of the world—move to Israel. And that every Christian should expedite their doing so.

The Christians also urged Israel to annex that portion of occupied Palestine called the West Bank, with its near one million Palestinian inhabitants. An Israeli Jew, seated in the audience, rose—before the motion was voted upon—to suggest that perhaps the language might be modified. He pointed out that an Israeli poll showed that one-third of the Israelis would be willing to trade territory seized in 1967 for peace with the Palestinians.

"We don't care what the Israelis vote!" declared van der Hoeven. "We care what God says! And God gave that land to the Jews!" After his impassioned outburst, the Christians by a nearly unanimous show of hands passed the resolution.

The Christians also urged that the United States and "all nations" legitimize former Prime Minister Begin's illegal annexation of Arab Jerusalem by moving their embassies from Tel Aviv to Jerusalem. The Christians "demanded" that the United States, West Germany and other European nations "desist from arming Israel's foes." They added that the United States should withhold military weapons promised to Egypt until "she fully honors her treaty obligations to establish normal relations with Israel, including trade and tourism."

We met in sessions for 12 hours a day on three consecutive days. I estimated that out of a total of 36 hours we were in session, the Christians who sponsored the Congress devoted less than one percent of the time to the message and meanings of Christ, while they devoted more than 99 percent of the time to politics. This was not surprising since the sponsors, although Christians, were first and foremost Zionists and therefore primarily interested in the political goals of Zionism.

Following the Basel meeting, I took a Swiss train to a small village near Berne called Wildersil and sat, outside a small hotel, in the sun, with an occasional glance to the snow-covered Jungfrau, reading books and essays on Zionism.

While Theodor Herzl generally is known as the father of political Zionism, he did not initiate or create the movement to encourage Jews to move to Palestine. English Protestant Christians did so three centuries before the first Jewish-Zionist Congress.

Before the Reformation, all Western Christians were Catholic and generally accepted a view taught by Saint Augustine and others that certain biblical passages should be interpreted allegorically— not literally. As an example, Jerusalem and Zion were heavenly, other-worldly—open to all of us, and not an actual place here on earth, to be inhabited exclusively by Jews.

By the 16th and 17th centuries, Christians for the first time were buying Bibles and interpreting Scripture for themselves. In doing so, they began to elevate the concept of Israel—and the Jews—as the key factors in Biblical prophecy.

Few scholars have examined why Christians somewhat suddenly began to support the idea that all Jews should move to Palestine—an idea that had not flourished in orthodox Christian theology. Or why Protestants began to write lengthy biblical prophecy tomes that gave the Jews, traditionally viewed as enemies of the church, a new Christian theological significance. After the Reformation, European Christians became more interested in the Jews and changed their attitudes toward them, some scholars tell us, because of developments in European international law which led to greater tolerance. Other scholars point to the expanded economic role that the Jews came to play in world trade. Some maintain that the Renaissance interest in Hebrew studies as well as Reformation theology, with its emphasis on the Old Testament, focused attention on the Jews, so much so that Judaic sects—or sects with strongly judaizing influences—emerged within English Protestant churches.

Some scholars have characterized the Reformation as a "hebraizing" or "judaizing" revival, with early Protestants accepting such features of the Judaic tradition as messianism (expecting a Messiah) and millenarianism (a rule of peace for a thousand years on this earth). It was during the Reformation that Protestant Christians accepted the Bible as constituting the supreme authority of belief as well as conduct. Instead of an infallible Church as represented by the Pope in Rome, the Protestants accepted an infallible Bible, which was now translated into the languages of ordinary people.

With the translation of the Scripture into the vernacular, the early Protestants turned to the Old Testament, known as the Jewish or Hebrew Bible, to familiarize themselves with the history, stories, traditions and laws of the Hebrews and the land of Palestine. They memorized the Old Testament stories and could recite passages by heart. And many Protestants began to think of Palestine as Jewish land.

The Protestants turned to the Old Testament not only as their most popular literature but also as their one source book for general historical knowledge. They thus reduced the total history of pre-Christian Palestine to those episodes including only the Hebrew presence. Vast numbers of Christians became conditioned to believe that nothing had happened in ancient Palestine except the hazy events half-concealed in murky legends and sparse historical narratives recorded in the Old Testament. Bible-loving Christians came to regard the Old Testament as the only history that mattered in the Middle East.

By the mid 1600s Protestants began to write treatises declaring that all Jews should leave Europe for Palestine. Oliver Cromwell, as Lord Protector of the newly established Puritan Commonwealth, declared that Jewish presence in Palestine would be the prelude to the Second Coming of Christ.

In 1655, German Protestant Paul Felgenhauever proclaimed that Jews at the Second Coming of Christ would recognize Jesus as their Messiah. The sign that would prove this, he wrote in *Good News for Israel*, would be "the permanent return of the Jews to their own country eternally bestowed upon them by God through the unqualified promise to Abraham, Isaac and Jacob."

In 1839, Lord Anthony Ashley Cooper, seventh Earl of Shaftsbury and known as the "Great Reformer" for his championing of more humane treatment of child labor, the mentally ill and prisoners, urged all Jews to emigrate to Palestine. In a published article, "State and Prospects of the Jews," he expressed concern over the "Hebrew race" but opposed the idea of assimilation and emancipation on the ground that Jews would always remain aliens in all countries where non-Jews resided.

Lord Shaftesbury saw Jews playing a stellar role in the "divine plan" of the Second Coming of Christ. As he interpreted Scripture, the Second Coming of Christ would transpire only with the Jews living in a restored and converted Israel.

Convinced that he should help God bring about the divine plan of moving all Jews to Palestine, Lord Shaftesbury made it his task to convince his fellow Englishmen that the Jews, "though admittedly a stiff-necked, dark-hearted people, and sunk in moral degradation, obduracy and ignorance of the Gospel"—were nevertheless vital to a Christian's hope of salvation.

The English lord did not bother to investigate whether Palestinians were then living in Palestine, nor did it concern him that the people and their land were not his to give away. He simply stated that the land of Palestine was available. As he put it, Palestine was "a country without a nation for a nation without a country," a phrase later used by Jewish Zionists as "A land without a people for a people without a land."

In his zeal to move Jews to an exclusively Jewish state, Lord Shaftesbury influenced his step-father-in-law, Lord Palmerston, Britain's Foreign Secretary, to open a British consulate in Jerusalem. In appointing devout evangelical William Young as first British Vice Consul to Jerusalem in 1839, the Foreign Secretary specifically stated that he should protect all the Jews residing in Palestine, which was then a part of the Ottoman Empire. In that year a total of 9,690 Jews lived in Palestine. They included both native Jews as well as foreign national Jews.

According to established treaty rights, British consular protection applied only to foreign national Jews residing in Palestine. Native Jews on the other hand were still under the sole jurisdiction of the Sultan as subjects of the Ottoman Empire. However, the British Vice Consul, wishing to "make the Hebrews in Palestine appreciate how kindly the British government was disposed toward them," extended protection to all Jews in Palestine.

The British had no more right to extend sovereignty over native Jews living in Palestine than France or Spain would have had to extend sovereignty over native Catholics living in Palestine. The British action not only was interference in the internal affairs of a foreign country, it also set a major cornerstone of Zionism: it affirmed the national unity of all Jewish people.

In 1841, Charles Henry Churchill, British staff officer serving in the Middle East, wrote to Moses Montefiore, President of the Jewish Board of Deputies in London: "I cannot conceal from you my most anxious desire to see your countrymen endeavor once more to resume their existence as a people. I consider the object to be perfectly obtainable. But two things are indispensably necessary. Firstly that the Jews themselves will take up the matter, universally and unanimously. Secondly that the European powers will aid them in their views."

In 1845, Edward L. Mitford of London's Colonial Office proposed "the establishment of the Jewish nation in Palestine, as a protected state under the guardianship of Great Britain," tutelage to be withdrawn once the Jews were able to take care of themselves. A Jewish state, he said, "would place us in a commanding position in the Levant from whence to check the process of encroachment, to overawe our enemies and, if necessary repel their advance."

However, Europe's Jews had little or no desire to leave their native lands and emigrate to Palestine.

For 150 years, Christians—for the most part in England, but also in other parts of Europe and later on, to a marked degree in America—were the only advocates of Zionism. Protestants acted on their own in insisting that Palestine belonged to the Jews—and in urging all Jews to go there and live separate from the Gentiles. For a century and a half, the Christians—leaders in the movement of Western imperialism—gained no support from Jews in their non-Jewish Zionism.

Christians in the forefront of this movement were, without exception, pious church-going Protestants. However, the terms Christian Zionist or Gentile Zionist can be misleading since it suggests a Zionism motivated by biblical or theological reasoning. Beyond the piety, writes Regina Sharif in *Non-Jewish Zionism*, the Christian Zionists held "political motivations," and these, she stresses, were from the beginning far more important than their religious beliefs.

Regardless of why Reformation Protestants supported the idea of an England and a Europe free of all Jews, many Jewish Zionists today say they are glad the Christians acted with such fervor. They credit Christian Zionism with helping modern Jewish Zionism achieve its goal—the creation of a Jewish state where only a Jew is welcomed as a citizen.

In a February 6, 1985, address on Christian Zionism at the National Prayer Breakfast for Israel, Israeli U.N. Ambassador Benjamin Netanyahu praised the "historical partnership that worked so well to fulfill the Zionist dream." Journalists, he said, in recent time "have made much of the support of evangelical Christians for Israel. Many have been puzzled and surprised by what they consider to be a new-found friendship. But for those who know the history of Christian involvement in Zionism, there is nothing either surprising or new about the steadfast support given to Israel by believing Christians all over the world . . .

"For what, after all, is Zionism?. . .

"There was an ancient yearning in our common tradition for the return of the Jews to the Land of Israel. And this dream, smoldering thoughout two millennia, finally burst forth in Christian Zionism . . . British and American writers, clerics, journalists, artists and statesmen all became ardent proponents of facilitating the return of the Jews to their desolate homeland.

"There was, for example, Lord Lindsay who wrote in the 1840s that the 'Jewish race, so wonderfully preserved, may yet have another stage of national existence open to them, may once more obtain possession of their native land.' And there was George Grawler, who in 1845 urged: 'Replenish the farms and fields of Palestine with the energetic people whose warmest affections are rooted in the soil.' "

Christian Zionism, Ambassador Netanyahu continued, was not only a current of idealism. Practical plans were actually drawn up for the return of the Jews. In 1848, Warder Cresson, the American Consul in Jerusalem, helped establish a Jewish settlement in the Valley of Refaim, supported by a joint Christian-Jewish society in England. And Claude Condor, an aide to Lord Kitchener, carried out an extensive survey of Palestine, concluding that "the country could be restored by the Jews to its ancient prosperity."

Christians had provided a "long, intimate and ultimately successful support" for Zionism, Netanyahu continued, a support that expressed itself in English literature such as George Eliot's influential novel on Zionism, *Daniel Deronda*, which predicted Jews would establish "a new Jewish polity, grand, simple, just, like the old—a republic where there is equality of protection, an equality which gave . . . more than the brightness of Western freedom amid the despotism of the East. For there will be a country in the East which carries the culture and the sympathy of every great nation in its bosom."

Christians, Netanyahu said, helped turn "a sheer fantasy" into a Jewish state. "Consider, for example, Edwin Sherman Wallace, the U.S. Consul in Palestine, who in 1898 wrote, 'The Land is waiting, the people are ready to come, and will come as soon as protection to life and property is assured . . . This must be accepted or the numerous prophecies that asserted so positively must be thrown out as worthless . . . (Yet) the present movements among Jews in many parts of the world indicate their belief in the prophetic assertions. Their eyes are turning toward the Land that once was theirs and their hearts are longing for the day when they as a people can dwell securely in it.'

"The writings of the Christian Zionists, British and American, directly influenced the thinking of such pivotal leaders as Lloyd George, Arthur Balfour and Woodrow Wilson at the beginning of this century," Netanyahu said. "These were all men versed in the Bible. These were men whose imagination was ignited by the dream of the great ingathering. And these were all men who had a crucial role in laying the political foundations, internationally, for the restoration of the Jewish State. Thus it was the impact of Christian Zionism on Western statesmen that helped modern Jewish Zionism achieve the rebirth of Israel.

"A sense of history, a sense of poetry, and a sense of morality imbued the Christian Zionists who more than a century ago began to write, and plan, and organize for Israel's restoration . . . So those who are puzzled by what they consider the new-found friendship between Israel and its Christian supporters reveal an ignorance of both. But we know better. We know the spiritual ties that link us so profoundly and so enduringly," Netanyahu concluded. "We know the historical partnership that worked so well to fulfill the Zionist dream."

Herzl's dream, however, was not spiritual. It was geographical, a dream for land, power and territory. This being so, many Jews have become disillusioned with political Zionism.

To take the land of Palestine with clear conscience, the Zionists had to assume that the people who owned the land were not there. Initially, political Zionists claimed that there were no Palestinians living in Palestine. Immigrant Jews were startled, however, to discover the other occupants of Palestine, the 93 percent indigenous populace. The Israeli writer Amos Elon relates that in 1897 one of Herzl's associates came crying to the Zionist leader:

"But there are Arabs in Palestine. I did not know that!"

"From the beginning of Zionism," writes the American Jewish writer I. F. Stone, "we have hated to admit that the Arabs were there. We knew they were there, but we pretended that they weren't. Imagine that you were a dentist or a doctor in Jerusalem or Haifa, or that you had a villa along the little Arab Riviera in Jaffa—there were some lovely Arab villas there. Or imagine that you were a farmer, or that you had a business, or that you went to school. Then, suddenly, everything was swept away. You lost your home, your business, your school, your country. You would feel bitter—there is nothing mysterious about that—and you would feel desperate."

Moshe Menuhin, father of violinist Yehudi Menuhin, said he moved to the newly-created Jewish state hoping to find a spiritual haven but discovered the Zionists were worshiping "not God but their own power." In 1981, in a personal letter to me, Menuhin, then 88, bemoaned "the tragic decadence" of prophetic Judaism that he said had been replaced by political Zionism.

In a Jerusalem *Post* interview, the noted American Jewish violinist Isaac Stern called Zionism and the Zionist state "my tarnished dream."

Mark Bruzonsky, a Washington, D. C., writer and computer specialist, also calls political Zionism a tarnished dream. Before breaking with Zionism, Bruzonsky had worked for Jewish Zionist organizations. "Being a liberal in politics, I viewed Zionism with varying degrees of enthusiasm, as the Jewish version of self-determination."

And what changed his mind about Zionism?

"Simple," he said, "I learned too much. I started reading. And I kept reading. A Jew is supposed to work for Zionism, but not read too much about it. A Jew is supposed to accept the history of Zionism but in fact not really study it."

How, I asked, is Zionism best defined?

"Some define Zionism as the end of exile and the ingathering of all Jews. Most Arabs define Zionism as a form of racist colonization. And delegates to the United Nations at one point voted to condemn Zionism as a form of racism. George Orwell said Zionism had the usual characteristics of a nationalist movement, 'but the American version of it seems to be more violent and malignant than the British.' And the British historian Toynbee defined Zionism as 'the worship of a false god'—an 'idolatrous religion.' "

What, I asked, was Bruzonsky's definition of Zionism?

"I term Zionism a political, expansionist, colonial-type movement that led to the creation of Israel, and I term the Zionist as one who accepts the rationale of Israel's actions, regardless of how dangerous or wrong they may be."

Then from his definition it was apparent that Christians could be classified as Zionists?

"Oh sure. Zionism would never have been started without Christians wanting to put Jews in a ghetto—called a Jewish state, exclusively for Jews. The tragedy is that after resisting the idea for about 200 years the Jews went along with it."

Just as early Christian Zionists urged European Jews to go to Palestine and take as much land as they could, so Christian Zionists such as Jerry Falwell urge Jews today to go beyond Palestine—and claim all the Arab lands that stretch from the River Euphrates on the east, west to the Nile River.

Falwell, on February 6, 1983, told the Tyler, Texas, *Courier Times-Telegram* that he favors Israelis taking portions of present day Iraq, Syria, Turkey, Saudi Arabia, Egypt, Sudan and all of Lebanon, Jordan and Kuwait. As far as the boundaries of mandated Palestine, it all belongs to the Jews, Falwell said, adding "God has blessed America because we have cooperated with God in protecting that which is precious to Him (Israel)."

It is because they know they have the support of some 40 million Christian evangelical-fundamentalists that American Jews such as

Andy Green move from the Bronx and at gunpoint take land from the Palestinians. "The Arabs have no claim to the land (Palestine)," Green, who moved to Israel in 1975 but still retains his U.S. passport, told Friedman in the *Village Voice* article. "It's our land, absolutely. It says so in the Bible. It's something that can't be argued. That's why I see no reason to sit down and talk with the Arabs about competing claims. Whoever is stronger will get the land."

According to the *Village Voice* article, Hanan Porat, a leading Gush intellectual, says: "Jewish sovereignty over Israel and the dream of the Priestly Kingdom and being a Holy Nation are preconditions for the world to become whole again. Unless these preconditions are met, there will be no peace."

All Zionists—Christians, Jews and most especially the leaders of the Jewish terrorist movements Kach and Gush Emunim—share Porat's mystical-messianic views. They see the Land of Israel as a moral absolute. Both Christian and Jewish Zionists insist that mysticism is a healthy part of their religious heritage. Rabbi Moshe Levinger, a ringleader for the terrorists convicted of plotting to kill Palestinian mayors and destroy the Dome of the Rock, defines Zionism for himself and countless others:

"Zionism is mysticism. Zionism will wither away if you cut it from its mystical-messianic roots. Zionism is a movement that does not think in rational terms—in terms of practical politics, international relations, world opinion, demography, social dynamics—but in terms of divine commandments. What matters only is God's promise to Abraham as recorded in the Book of Genesis."

The Andy Green, Hanan Porat and Rabbi Levinger quotes are all taken from the forementioned *Village Voice* article, "Inside the Jewish Terrorist Underground," by Robert Friedman.

A MARRIAGE
OF CONVENIENCE

Why Israel Sought the Alliance With the New Christian Right

Perhaps I am somewhat typical of many Christians who grew up before there was an Israel on our maps. All Christians I knew in the year of 1948 welcomed the creation of a Jewish state with our prayers and admiration. We read and heard and knew only good aspects about Israel.

And my image of Israelis perhaps was somewhat typical. I viewed them as a hard-working, fair-minded people, toiling the fields, making the desert bloom, a God-fearing, peace loving people. In short, I identified with them, as perhaps so many of other millions of Americans did, because they seemed so much like us— "pioneers" or descendents of pioneers who, one was led to believe, created a new and better world from what many perceived was a backward region of Orientals.

I did not personally know Israelis in the 1950s and 1960s. I gained my perception of Israel and Israelis largely from liberal American Jews who had done so much to bring the Jewish state into existence. I learned about the first settlements of Jews in Palestine through the books and other writings of early prophetic Jews, whose conceptions of a Jewish homeland had been nourished in the richest of ideals. The early Zionists voiced their dedication to an Israel of socialistic justice for all its citizens and of peace with their Arab neighbors into whose world they had moved.

Just as liberal Jews such as Ha'am, Buber, Magnes and Menuhin recognized that Palestinians (Christians and Muslims) were indigenous to the land, and identified with the suffering of Palestinians who were made homeless, so liberal American Jews, possibly more than any other U.S. group, identified with and worked to alleviate the suffering of other Americans, such as blacks and Indians who have known discrimination. Liberal American Jews had strong ties with U.S. labor and were often identified as a strong pillar in the northern liberal establishment, with which the Christian Right often takes issue.

The most active and best known Jewish liberals live in the Northeast and in major urban centers, in particular New York City. They had little interest in or knowledge of evangelical-fundamentalists, who were largely in the South, Midwest and West. The two groups have had little or nothing in common. Many Southern fundamentalists were parochial and openly racist, convinced that as white Anglo-Saxon Protestants they were superior to blacks, Indians, Catholics, Chinese, Japanese, Hindus, Muslims and Jews.

Millions of American WASPS had been bequeathed this legacy of narrow-mindedness and hate. Right-wing Christians such as Gerald Winrod preached and published through his *The Defender* magazine a blatant anti-Jewish doctrine. Other right-wing Christians including Gerald L. K. Smith, Willian Dudley Pelley, William Kullgren, Wesley Swift and William L. Blessing preached that a "Christian" America would be better without the Jews.

As regards a Jew, white evangelical-fundamentalists have often alleged their superiority not, as is the case of the black Christian, because of fairer skin, but because they, as Christians had accepted Jesus Christ and were thereby saved, while the Jew, along with all who refuse to accept the divinity of Jesus Christ, was not.

The Christian fundamentalist therefore believes he should save the Jew from his Judaism by showing him that Christianity is the true fulfillment of Judaism. Since American Jews were repelled by this Christian proselytizing, they kept their distance from fundamentalists.

Besides the geographical separation between Jews and fundamentalists, there were the traditional theological and ideological differences on social issues. Liberal Eastern establishment Jews and Gentiles alike recoiled at the aggressive conservative social agenda of many evangelical-fundamentalists including their support for more nuclear bombs, prayer in school and anti-abortion measures. Liberal American Jews had early on joined with liberal American

Catholics and Protestants in supporting measures that would heal and be constructive, and this became increasingly true after the creation of Israel.

From 1948 to 1967, American Jewish leaders met regularly and harmoniously with leaders of both the U.S. Catholic Conference of Bishops (representing about 40 million Catholics) and the National Council of Churches (representing another 40 million Christians). The liberal Protestant churches, including among others Presbyterians, Episcopalians and United Methodists, were the first to include studies on anti-Semitism in their religious textbooks during the 1940s and 1950s. They advocated separation of church and state and encouraged political justice for minority groups—positions shared by most Jews in America.

In the 1960s, while working for three years at the White House, I observed how President Johnson moved civil rights legislation through Congress to help end discrimination toward blacks. I noted that Jews were the strongest supporters of these bills. Later when I wrote books dealing with the plight of blacks, Indians and undocumented Mexican workers, I learned that liberal Jews gave the greatest support for my books. This was only natural as the overwhelming thrust of Jewish thought in America for several decades had been liberal.

This being true, when and why did American Jews and Israeli Jews seek an alliance with ultra-conservative evangelical-fundamentalists such as Jerry Falwell? Since it is not a mutually shared relation that brings the evangelical-fundamentalists and the Jews together, what does? The TV evangelists repeatedly tell us that a Jewish state provides them a place where they will meet Jesus and enjoy eternal bliss. But knowing that Jerry Falwell, Jimmy Swaggart, Pat Robertson and most major TV evangelists believe every Jew will be either killed or converted to Christ, why should Jews seek to collaborate with them? Why would Jews set aside deeply held theological and humanitarian beliefs to establish an alliance with right-wing fundamentalists?

Rabbi Marc R. Tanenbaum, a well-known Jewish liaison with American Christians, said Israel and U.S. Jewish supporters of Israel sought the new alliance because they had been "abandoned" by liberal Christians, and in particular by the National Council of

Churches (NCC). Tanenbaum summarized the change in this way:

"Since the 1967 war, the Jewish community has felt abandoned by Protestants, by groups clustered around the National Council of Churches, which, because of sympathy with third-world causes, gave an impression of support for the PLO. There was a vacuum in public support to Israel that began to be filled by the fundamentalist and evangelical Christians."

However, NCC leaders deny Tanenbaum's charge that the Council "abandoned" the American Jewish community and Israel. I talked with one well-known NCC leader, Dr. Tracey E. Jones, Jr., who has maintained a long and close association with Rabbi Tanenbaum. "The NCC in its actual policies and positions remained decidedly pro-Israel," said Dr. Jones, former general secretary of the United Methodist Church's Board of Global Ministries and chairman of the NCC's Middle East Panel. However, there were changes taking place, as the Reverend L. Humphrey Walz of Janesville, Wisconsin, a Presbyterian minister and long active with the council, explained:

"A number of the globally alert Protestant leaders had become involved with the plight of homeless Palestinians and included them in their pleas for support for the destitute all over the world. Their views were consonant with those of the Geneva-based World Council of Churches, representing more than 300 churches of the Protestant, Anglican, Orthodox and Old Catholic traditions from over 100 countries.

"The NCC meanwhile was attempting to formulate statements that showed an awareness of Palestinian suffering. All of the NCC leaders were careful to make such statements as fair and as conciliatory as possible toward all parties to the conflict. NCC leaders continued to strive for a stand on Middle East issues that was in the best interest of all, including Israel, but the American Zionist establishment blasts any such even-handedness as insufficiently supportive and therefore antagonistic," Dr. Walz said.

Additionally, I interviewed Dr. Frank Maria of Warner, New Hampshire, whose lifelong work has been in human relations and communications and who originated the proposal of "Common Denominator Diplomacy," with precepts that led to America's Peace Corps and People-to-People programs. Serving on the governing board of the National Council of Churches, he championed what he termed God's Peace Plan—based upon the ethics and spiritual insights of the three monotheistic religions of the area. What of the charge, I asked Dr. Maria, made by Rabbi Tanenbaum that the NCC had abandoned pro-Israel supporters?

"Previous to the 1967 war, Rabbi Tanenbaum could boast, 'The NCC never makes a statement without my approval,' " Dr. Maria said. "I would not want to say that the NCC governing board was a rubber stamp for Israel, but it was responsive to the pressures and concerns of the American Jewish community and less relevant in its responses to the plight of Christians and Muslims in the Middle East.

"The NCC did not 'abandon' Rabbi Tanenbaum and other supporters of Israel. But rather Israel and its supporters in this country decided they could get other help—from the evangelical-fundamentalists—and they deemed this more valuable."

But why, I wondered, would Israel consider evangelical-fundamentalists such as Falwell more valuable than Dr. Tracey Jones and others within the NCC?

"Everything changed with the 1967 war," Dr. Maria, whose parents were born in Syria, said. "Americans in general got a different perspective of Israel. Until 1967, they saw Israel as 'little David' arrayed against overpowering Arab Goliaths. Then suddenly the Israelis attacked their neighbors. They struck the Egyptian air force by surprise, destroying it on the ground in a Pearl Harbor-type attack. Israelis marched into the Sinai, seized the West Bank, Arab Jerusalem, the Gaza strip and the Golan Heights.

"Every day during the 1967 war, I saw on television the Israelis killing Egyptians as if they were ants. And I saw Israelis on the Golan Heights killing Syrians who looked like my late father and brother," Dr. Maria continued. "I watched Israeli soldiers with bayonets push Palestinian women and children across the Allenby bridge into Jordan. I saw my own mother and sister in those women. Yet, I knew that as Arabs were being oppressed or killed by the Israelis, many Americans, Christians and Jews, sat by their TVs applauding.

"I was born in this country, and I had all of my life tried to live as a good American. Since 1942, I had worked with organizations involved in humanitarian, educational and political activities to help effect a pro-American, pro-peace policy in the Middle East, which I term America's priority world challenge. But knowing that Americans were applauding the killing of Christians and Muslims because they perceived all Arabs as 'bad'—this became my darkest moment. My inspiration to work within the Christian churches came from this moment of deep despair."

Dr. Maria called other American Christian leaders to a 1967 Boston conference and they petitioned President Johnson to order Israel's withdrawal from the West Bank, Arab Jerusalem, Gaza and the Golan Heights.

"That did not happen. But at least we began to make some Americans realize there were injustices which our government was supporting. At one point," Maria said "when an Israeli leader asked President Johnson to recognize the territories seized in 1967 from Arabs as part of Israel, the President replied, 'You are asking me to recognize your borders. You have never defined the borders of Israel.' "

The "borders of Israel" is the subject that has engaged the United Nations more than any other single issue. It was the U.N. that recommended creating Israel as a Jewish Palestine along with an Arab Palestine, and defined Israel's borders in 1948. Since then, Israel has consistently changed those borders—printing its own maps and including the lands which some of its leaders, such as Menachem Begin, said God gave to the Jews. No other nation in the world has recognized or accepted the borders that Israel gives itself.

World leaders contend "we must abide by 242"—referring to a resolution passed in the United Nations. A British representative to the United Nations, Lord Caradon, put together the resolution numbered 242 to which world leaders have consistently referred as the best basis for peace in the Middle East.

In a 1982 visit to London, I met with the distinguished, personable Lord Caradon, who first went to Jerusalem in the late 1920s, to serve as the most junior cadet in the British Mandatory Government of Palestine. Over cups of tea, he told me about those early days:

"In the week of my arrival I witnessed the Wailing Wall riots of 1929. Subsequently I served in Palestine during the Arab rebellion of the late 1930s in days of violent demonstrations. I was in Nablus nearly ten years and in Amman for three years. I once walked alone from Sidon to Damascus, going over the top of Mount Hermon. And I was very kindly received by all the villagers. It was nice to walk in the area. And I knew every village north of Jerusalem. I used to set out every Monday morning with an agricultural inspector and away we'd go. You could stop in any village you liked, they were glad to have you."

Lord Caradon reviewed the intervening years of the holocaust in Germany, and explained how the Western world, feeling sympathy for European Jews, carved out of Palestine a homeland for the victims of Nazism. "The Arabs have been made to pay for Hitler's crimes," he said. He thinks the Israelis and Arabs might have lived in peace had there been justice in those years for the Palestinians. "They became more destitute after the 1967 war." The United Nations charter as well as other international laws, including those known as the Geneva Accords, all state that no nation can legally retain territories seized militarily.

Building on these international laws, Caradon formulated a resolution (242) that said every nation in the Middle East, including Israel, had a right to exist in peace within secure boundaries, and second, that Israel should return to Arab control all the territories captured by Israel in the 1967 war. Hugh Caradon dramatically told how, once the issue came to a vote, he saw the hand of the Soviet representative Vasilily Vasil-yerich Kuznetsov being raised in favor of the resolution, as well as the hand of the American U.N. representative, Arthur Goldberg, voting in its behalf. Thus in November 1967 the U.N. Security Council passed Resolution 242—and did so unanimously.

"It has now been almost two decades since the resolution was passed," commented Lord Caradon. "And Israel has not enjoyed a day of peace."

And why was this?

"The United States has not demanded or even encouraged Israel to withdraw from its illegally held territories. Rather the United States has supplied Israel total financial and moral support for its continued defiance of the U.N. requirements of returning the territories."

Lord Caradon then concluded: "Resolution 242 is important because it speaks of the essential necessity of Israeli withdrawal from Arab lands. If you can get withdrawal by the Israeli military forces, everything else can happen."

In a lengthy analysis paper prepared for Israel and American Jewish leaders, evangelical lay leader Douglas Krieger of Denver, Colorado, points out that as a consequence of its 1967 war of aggression, Israel faced two choices: to seek peace by withdrawing from "territory acquired by war", to use the language of the U.N. Charter and Resolutions 242 and 338. Or to continue reliance upon ever greater military strength.

"If the Israelis took the second choice and continued their militaristic aggrandizement—which Krieger, as a dispensationalist urged them to do—then the Israelis and American Jews would face the danger of an outbreak of anti-Semitism.

Because of Israel's military seizure of Arab lands, "a rise of anti-Semitism could possibly surge in the West." This could be prevented, however, Krieger said, through its alliance with the New Christian Right. He reminded Israeli and American Jewish leaders that evangelical-fundamentalists, like the Orthodox Jews, had a fascination with the land promised Abraham and his seed. And that Israel could use the evangelical-fundamentalists to project through their vast radio and television networks an image of Israel that Americans would like, accept and support.

Moreover, Krieger said, the Religious Right could sell the Americans on the idea that God wanted a militant, militarized Israel. And that the more militant Israel became, the more supportive and ecstatic in its support the U.S. Religious Right would become.

In 1967 the National Council of Churches called for the end of Israeli occupation of Arab lands. This was carried forward especially by the peace churches in the Council—including the Quakers, Mennonites and Church of the Brethren as well as the Presbyterians and the Methodists, who over the years had become increasingly emphatic in urging study of the Palestinian-Israeli conflict.

The NCC opened offices in Washington, D. C., and occasionally their members talked with senators and representatives on Middle

East issues or testified before congressional committees on conditions of the Palestinians in Gaza and the West Bank. And mainline Christian church publications have in a few instances printed articles that give their readers both sides of the Israeli-Palestinian conflict.

After the Antiochian church presented a resolution on "Violations of Human Rights and International Law by Israel" that called for a "cut-off of U.S. aid," the National Council of Churches sent a delegation to the West Bank to study the reported violations. On the basis of numerous interviews with people from every walk of life, the NCC then issued a statement in 1980 criticizing Israeli occupation policies and supporting a separate Palestinian state in Gaza and the West Bank. The World Council of Churches at its 1983 meeting in Vancouver passed a similar resolution. Meanwhile the National Catholic Conference of Bishops as early as 1974 had passed resolutions urging greater attention to Palestinian rights and the creation of a Palestinian state.

But overall, Israel's continued illegal occupation of Arab territories received scant attention from the vast majority of liberal Christian Americans. They tended to remain pro-Israel on Middle East issues. However, while Israel's retention of Arab territories did not noticeably change the perception of the state held by most liberal Christians, a hint of possible change was enough to disturb many Zionists. "Not surprisingly," noted Leon Hader in the Jerusalem *Post*, "they (the mainline Christian leaders) perceived Israel as a 'racist' and 'imperalist' state."

Even if this were true—and NCC leaders insist that it was not—the Israeli and American Jewish leaders had decided that if they lost the support of the NCC entirely, they would suffer no great loss.

And this was true for three reasons: First, the Israeli and American Jewish leaders were reasonably certain the mainline church leaders would not represent a strong voice against their occupation of Arab lands, which in fact, they did not. The Zionists could feel sure that even if individual liberal Protestant and Catholic leaders deplored the suffering of Palestinians and might on a rare occasion mention it, the issue for them was of no greater importance than a host of other issues, such as South African apartheid, the arms race or violation of human rights in Central America.

Meanwhile NCC and other liberal church leaders maintain the closest of friendships with Jewish supporters of Israel. In most U.S. cities, they serve with American Jewish leaders on city councils, as well as on hospital, university and community welfare boards. And when U.S. Christian ministers and Jewish rabbis meet to promote understanding among Christians and Jews in America, they almost invariably ignore the plight of Christians and Muslim Arabs in lands occupied by Israeli Jews.

Jewish Zionist leaders preferred to switch alliances from liberal to conservative Christians for a second reason: they would gain in fervent support. The NCC represents about 40 million Christians. The evangelical-fundamentalist churches represent an equal number. But if one of the 40 million liberal Christians affiliated with the NCC spoke out against the Israeli seizure of Arab lands, this one voice would hardy matter. It would be insignificant compared with the 40 million evangelical-fundamentalists who fervently believe God Himself wants Israel to have any and all of the Arab lands it can capture.

Israel and American Jewish leaders recognized that there is nothing in mainline Christianity that corresponds to the militant zealotry of the fundamentalists. For them Israel is an intrinsically religious concern, tied up with their own salvation. Of all foreign policy issues, they place the highest priority on Israel. For this reason, they tend to give total, unquestioning support to the Zionist state.

Then there's a third reason why pro-Israel supporters turned to a strict or what is called muscular Christianity: many leaders in both groups believe in more arms, bigger armies, more bombs and achieving goals through military power.

As Israel, beginning in 1967, locked itself into a muscular embrace with the Christian Right, and did so pragmatically, it moved many leading U.S. Jewish Zionists to do the same. Nathan Perlmutter of the Anti-Defamation League of B'nai B'rith provides us with the most clearcut explanation of why U.S. Jews began embracing fundamentalists. First, he explains he feels himself a somewhat typical American Jew in that he weighs every issue in life by one measure: "Is it good for the Jews? This question satisfied, I proceed to the secondary issues."

In the case of Jerry Falwell, liberal Jews should support him
because he supports Israel. That, for Perlmutter, is the primary
issue. Liberal Jews may not agree with Falwell's domestic policies
on more nuclear weapon bombs, abortion or prayer in schools. But,
contends Perlmutter, there are secondary issues. In his book, *The
Real Anti-Semitism in America,* Perlmutter writes:
   "Jews can live with all the domestic priorities of the Christian
Right on which liberal Jews differ so radically because none of these
concerns is as important as Israel."
   Perlmutter recognizes that evangelical-fundamentalists interpret
Scripture as saying all Jews eventually must accept Jesus Christ or
be killed in the Battle of Armageddon. But, meanwhile, he says,
"we need all the friends we have to support Israel . . . If the
Messiah comes, on that day we'll consider our options. Meanwhile,
let's praise the Lord and pass the ammunition."
   Increasingly, other Jewish leaders have taken this same approach. Irving Kristol, a leading spokesman for New York's Jewish
intellectual community, urges American Jews to form a closer
alliance with Jerry Falwell and other right-wing conservatives.
Liberalism, writes Kristol in a widely-publicized July 1984 *Commen-
tary* essay, "is very much on the defensive," and Jews should move
away from it. "We are constrained to take our allies where and how
we find them."
   American Jews, he believes, have one overriding priority: Israel.
Since Falwell and the Moral Majority support Israel, American Jews
should in turn overwhelmingly support the neo-conservatives. For
Kristol, a Zionist state becomes the ultimate moral absolute, the
foundation of all other moral principles. He writes:
   "If one had informed American Jews 15 years ago that there
was to be a powerful revival of Protestant fundamentalism as a
political as well as religious force, they would surely have been
alarmed, since they would have assumed that any such revival might
tend to be anti-Semitic and anti-Israel. But the Moral Majority is
neither."
   Rather, Kristol, professor of social thought at New York University's Graduate School of Business Administration, sees the Moral
Majority as "strongly pro-Israel." To be sure, he adds, occasionally
a fundamentalist preacher will say that God does not hear the

prayers of a Jew. But "after all, why should Jews care about the theology of a fundamentalist preacher when they do not for a moment believe that he speaks with any authority on the question of God's attentiveness to human prayer? And what do such theological abstractions matter as against the mundane fact that the same preacher is vigorously pro-Israel?"

Kristol urges Jews to ask themselves the question: How significant would it be for American Jews if the Moral Majority were anti-Israel? "The answer is easy and inescapable: it would be of major significance. Indeed, it would generally be regarded by Jews as a very alarming matter."

True, Kristol writes, the Moral Majority is committed to a set of social issues—school prayer, anti-abortion, the relation of church and state in general—that tend to evoke a hostile reaction among most (though not all) American Jews. To balance the pros and cons of the matter, Kristol says that "the social issues of the Moral Majority are meeting with practically no success, whereas anti-Israel sentiment has been distinctly on the rise, and the support of the Moral Majority could, in the near future, turn out to be decisive for the very existence of the Jewish state. This is the way the Israeli government has struck its own balance vis-a-vis the Moral Majority, and it is hard to see why American Jews should come up with a different bottom line."

As regards international law, "no single ethnic or religious group in the United States has produced such a disproportionate number of scholars in the field of international law as have Jews." But, says Kristol, Jews should not remain loyal to those "grandiose principles" since Israel from time to time must break international laws and decide for itself what is legal and moral, based on one yardstick: what is good for the Jews.

"When Israel bombed and destroyed the Iraqi nuclear reactor most American Jews realized that this was a sensible thing to do and that there was nothing 'illegal' or 'immoral' about the act," writes Kristol.

In a world "rife with conflict and savagery," Kristol urges American Jews to be more embracing of the Moral Majority's social issues. American Jews "really do need to revise their thinking about some, at least, of these controversial social issues, even from the point of view of expediency. Moreover, it is becoming ever more clear that it is time they did so in any case, Moral Majority or no Moral Majority.

"Ever since the holocaust and the emergence of the state of Israel, American Jews have been reaching toward a more explicit and meaningful Jewish identity and have been moving away from the universalist secular humanism that was so prominent a feature of their prewar thinking."

As relatively new immigrants, "Jews found liberal opinion and liberal politicians more congenial in their attitudes, more sensitive to Jewish concerns." But, asks Kristol, "is there any point in Jews hanging on, dogmatically and hypocritically, to their opinions of yesteryear when it is a new era we are confronting?"

The new era will, in Kristol's opinion, be more conservative, and Jews can provide some of that leadership. The liberal consensus and the liberal coalition "that have dominated American politics since the inauguration of Franklin D. Roosevelt are disintegrating—at least so far as Jews are concerned." Can anyone doubt, Kristol asks, that under a liberal Democratic president "our next ambassador to the UN will be more like Andrew Young than Jeane Kirkpatrick?"

The liberal coalition is withdrawing from Jewish interests, Kristol writes, pointing to "the increasing and tragic polarization between blacks and Jews" and the changes within the trade unions. The current head of the AFL-CIO, Lane Kirkland, is a liberal and has worked with Jews, but "one can already see the ground shifting beneath his feet. It is, so far as American Jews are concerned, an ominous shift," Kristol warns.

So-called "Jewish unions" are disappearing. "The Amalgamated Clothing Workers, the International Ladies Garment Workers, the American Federation of Teachers still have Jewish leaders with close ties to the Jewish community. But their membership is already overwhelmingly black, Hispanic and Oriental, and future leaders will have no reason to be especially concerned with Jewish issues."

Organized labor, Kristol says, is moving away from the nonpolitical tradition of Samuel Gompers and is developing closer ties with the Democratic party. "As this happens, the unions themselves naturally take on the ideological coloration of their political allies.

If one wants to get a sense of what this can mean, one has simply to look at the 'educational materials' prepared by the National Education Association—once a professional association, now more a union—and observe how 'fair' it is to the PLO, how cooly skeptical it is of Israel's virtues."

The media also fail to be always pro-Israel. "In Britain, France, Germany, Italy, the media are even more highly critical of Israel, compassionate toward the PLO."

Kristol sees these changes in trade unions and the media as drifts toward liberalism, but he adds "liberalism's leftward drift is going no place while conservative and neoconservative politics are gaining momentum. Thus, American Jews should join the ultra-right." Everyone is headed in that direction, the movement is "against the liberal economic and political order and the liberal ideal of self-government." In this "real world" Jews are better off to back the ultra-conservatives. After all, Kristol concludes, it is better to back winners, not losers.

Alexander M. Schindler, a Reform rabbi and president of the Union of American Hebrew Congregations, believes American Jews "do ourselves irreparable harm when we permit our Jewishness to consist almost entirely of a vicarious participation in the life of Israel." Yet, he adds, "Most Jewish leaders are willing to forgive anything as long as they hear a good word about Israel."

Jacques Torczyner, an executive of the American sector of the World Zionist Organization, went further, stating it was natural for Zionists to embrace the New Christian Right. "We (the Jews) have, first of all, to come to the conclusion that the right-wing reactionaries are the natural allies of Zionism, not the liberals."

Alleck Resnick, president of the Zionist Organization of America, made clear he also supports the Jewish-fundamentalist alliance. "We welcome, accept and greet such Christian support for Israel without involving ourselves in their domestic agenda," Resnick told ZOA's June 1984 Presidential Leadership Conference in Jerusalem. Another speaker, Israel's Evangelical Liaison Harry Hurwitz, who works out of the Prime Minister's office, stressed that Israel welcomes right-wing evangelical support. He declared: "Christian fundamentalists are by and large supporters of Israel and we are not selective when it comes to mobilizing support."

Recognizing the importance of its alliance with the Christian fundamentalists, the Rabbinical Council appointed Rabbi Abner Weiss as its liaison to the New Christian Right and sponsored a Houston gathering of nearly 100 Orthodox Jews and evangelical-fundamentalists.

American Jewish leaders supporting an alliance with the New Christian Right include Rabbi Seymour Siegel of the Jewish Theological Seminary (Conservative), Rabbi Joshua Haberman of the Washington Hebrew Congregation (Reform), Rabbi Jacob Bronner, Executive Director of the Belz Hasidic Community, Dr. Harold Jacobs, President of the National Council of Young Israel (Orthodox), and Rabbi David Panitz of the Anti-Defamation League of B'nai B'rith.

In summation, the words of Jewish and Christian Right leaders tell us that they formed an alliance because they both want and strive for many of the same goals. Leaders in both camps favor unlimited military buildup of nuclear weapons and other armaments in both countries. Israel reportedly has as many as 20 nuclear weapons, and evangelical-fundamentalists with whom I talked said they wished the Israelis had more. Both Israeli Right and Christian Right leaders are nationalistic, militaristic, each with a dogma that demands the highest priority in their lives—a dogma centered around Israel and a cult of land.

Israel's evolution into a colonial and military power as well as its alliance with ultra-right Christians leaves many American liberal Jews feeling ambivalent and uncomfortable. "The overwhelming thrust of Jewish thought and writing in America these past several decades has been liberal, notably more so than in the population at large," Irving Howe and Bernard Rosenberg noted in *The New Conservatives*. Yet the U.S. Jewish liberals, the authors add, are now confused and Israel is at the heart of their confusion.

"The paradox that must be recognized is that insofar as Israel functions—must function—as a state dealing with other states, its impact upon American Jews is—perhaps must be—conservative."

A few American Jews have decried the growing trend of American Jewish leaders to place the cult of Israel above all else. Roberta Strauss Feuerlicht, born in Brooklyn of Orthodox Jewish parents, warns that American Jews have turned to worship a false god of Zionism, and in doing so they have relegated "much of the money and all of the power of the American Jews" to a small oligarchy of Jewish men.

In a superbly researched book, *The Fate of the Jews,* Feuerlicht points out that the first great contribution of Judaism was moral law, that the glory of the Judaism was not in its kings but in its prophets. Tourists, she reminds us, flock to the ancient fortress of Masada, site of a mass suicide by Jews to avoid capture, and Israeli servicemen are brought there to vow that Masada will never fall again.

But God ordered Jews not to die but to live, and she quotes God's injunction, "I have set before thee life and death . . . therefore choose life." Yet, she adds, Israelis, by putting their faith in armies and weapons and by honoring generals rather than prophets, are choosing not life—but death.

And she warns, those who make a cult of Israel are pushing us all in that direction.

What Israel Gains
from the Alliance

Money

Israel's three political goals in the United States might be summarized as follows: it wants money, it wants a U.S. Congress to rubber-stamp its political goals, and it wants exclusive, and total control over Jerusalem. The New Christian Right helps Israel in all three of these goals.

First, let us consider money. How much do we give? And is our money in the form of grants or loans, with interest paid, or is it an outright gift?

On the 1985 Falwell tour, I discussed U.S. aid to Israel with an Israeli, Hebrew University Professor Israel Shahak, chairman of the Israeli League for Human and Civil Rights. A survivor of the Bergen-Belsen concentration camp and a critic of Israel's expansionist policies, Dr. Shahak came to the Plaza hotel where the Falwell group was staying, and he and I talked over cups of coffee in the hotel's lobby-restaurant. After preliminary greetings, Dr. Shahak turned his attention to U.S. aid to Israel, saying that in 1985 the American taxpayers sent $5 billion to Israel.

"This means that you Americans send the equivalent of $1,700 to each Israeli man, woman and child, or, to put it another way, you send nearly $8,000 annually to each Israeli family of five. You give us about $14 million a day, 365 days a year, with no strings attached. You do not expect us to pay interest on this money, nor do you ask that we repay the capital. You make your billions an outright gift.

"Some of us in Israel as well as a few American friends, Jews and Christians, question whether the huge amount of aid is helping Israel in the long run. I feel that giving billions of dollars to Israel is the same as giving more narcotics to an addict. America does nothing to encourage us to take charge of our own lives, our own destinies.

"The nature of Zionism has always been to seek a protector, a provider. In the beginning, the political Zionists looked to England and it provided. Now the Zionists look to and depend entirely on the United States. And they have formed this alliance with the New Christian Right, which endorses any military or criminal action Israel takes," Shahak said. He concluded by saying that even if a few Israelis and Americans realize the unlimited flow of billions of U.S. dollars actually cripples and harms Israel, "the alliance of the Israeli Right with the Christian Right will insist that you Americans continue to send an ever-increasing amount of aid."

Shortly after talking with the Israeli professor, I, along with others on the Falwell tour boarded a plane bound for New York. I sat next to Marvin, in his late 60s, and retired as a top executive of a Kansas flour milling company. We discussed America's alarming deficit, our imbalance of trade and our inability to feed and educate our people, and eventually we turned to our aid to Israel. I mentioned my talk with Professor Shahak and his having said that Americans annually send about five billion dollars to Israel.

And what, I asked, if Israel says it needs 10 billion dollars?

"We will send it," Marvin said.

And if Israel wants 15 billion?

"It would need it, or Israel would not ask," he said.

"And we will send it. God would want us to do so. No question about that."

Back home in Washington, D.C., I met with Paul Findley, former ranking Republican on the House Foreign Affairs subcommittee. He served as a U.S. representative from the same Illinois district that in 1846 sent Abraham Lincoln to Congress, and was in the nation's capital promoting his book, *They Dare to Speak Out*, dealing with Congress and the Israeli lobby. Over lunch, I told the distinguished, silver-haired, 64-year-old Findley what Marvin and other fundamentalists had told me: that the U.S. would and should give any amount of money that Israel wants.

Was it also Findley's opinion, I asked, that the American people would vote ever-increasing billions to Israel?

"The American people themselves do not have a chance to vote on the issue where billions of dollars earmarked as foreign aid will go. The Senate and the House of Representatives do that," Findley reminded me. "And in the case of aid packages to Israel, the Congress without exception votes overwhelmingly to send the amount of money that Israel says it needs.

"Congress may and does question aid it sends to any other country or aid for school lunches, pregnant mothers or to bolster our Social Security programs. But Congress always votes for aid to Israel. Israel, with only four million people, is by far the chief beneficiary of our aid program—it gets about one-third of all U.S. foreign aid."

Had Findley ever seen an Israeli aid request voted down in his 22 years on Capital Hill?

"No, it's never happened," he said. "In this regard, the Israeli lobby writes its own ticket. It wins all its requests for money. With the exception of only two or three bills dealing with U.S. sale of arms to Arab countries, the Israeli lobby says what it wants, and Congress votes to give it. It has, you might say, generally dictated our Middle East policies."

Since the pro-Israel lobby has traditionally worked with American Democrats and gotten what it wanted in Congress, what did Israel gain, I asked, in forming an alliance with the New Christian Right?

"The Israeli lobby is shrewd enough to keep its old, traditional liberal Democratic friends, while at the same time it makes new friends among the conservative and ultra-conservative Republicans, whose constituents in many instances are followers of Jerry Falwell and other New Christian Right leaders. With both the liberal Democrats and conservatives in their pockets, the Israeli lobby will be able to swing unanimous or near unanimous votes for the Middle East policies it wants."

On the 1983 tour with Falwell, I recalled to Findley, the Lynchburg preacher told a Jerusalem press conference the day would come in America when "no candidate unfriendly to Israel can be elected to any U.S. office." Did Findley believe that?

"That's very much the case today with the U.S. Congress," he said. "And it is not a question of being 'unfriendly.' The lobby does not want a legislator to say there are two sides to the Arab-Israeli conflict. Rather, it says any candidate must be one hundred percent on Israel's side or you will be defeated." Asked if he could give examples, he replied:

"Chuck Percy and I are good examples."

And why, specifically, had he—Findley—lost his Congressional seat?

"I called for an even-handed approach to the Middle East problem. But the pro-Israel lobby interpreted my saying there were two sides to the Arab-Israeli conflict as criticism of Israel. This lobby wants to stamp out all criticism of Israel in Congress, in the press and in academia. And they are willing to stifle free speech to do it. To them, criticizing Israel or even mentioning the word Palestinian is tantamount to anti-Semitism.

"Thirty-one Jewish political action committes or PACs gave $104,325 to my politically little-known opponent. At this time, that was the only race in which combined giving by such PACs had exceeded $100,000. I think I can safely say that if Israel's lobby had left me alone, I would have won reelection."

And what had Charles Percy, former Senate Foreign Relations Committee chairman, done to incur the wrath of the Israeli lobby?

"He voted yes on the 1981 sale of the airborne warning and control system aircraft—the AWACS—to Saudi Arabia. And that vote probably cinched his demise—even though he had been supportive of all aid bills to Israel. The network of Jewish PACs voted $1.82 million to 1984 Senate candidates and 44 percent of that went to opponents of five senators—among them Percy—who voted for the AWACS sale.

"The Jewish PACs gave $329,825 for one purpose: to defeat Senator Percy. In addition, Michael R. Goland, a California real estate investor with ties to one of the Jewish PACs, spent $1.1 million in an 'independent' television, direct-mail and billboard campaign against Senator Percy."

It was generally known, I suggested, that the Israeli Zionists wanted Percy out. But how, specifically, had they benefited from their alliance with the New Christian Right?

"They benefited especially in this instance.

"The Israeli lobby worked with Falwell's associate Richard A. Viguerie, one of the founders of the Moral Majority. And Viguerie came out with a statement that he wanted to see Chuck Percy defeated." Thus, concluded Findley, "the ultra-conservatives Viguerie and Falwell threw all their support back of a liberal Democrat, Paul Simon, who being 100 percent pro-Israel, was the candidate favored by the Israeli lobby."

The Israeli lobby used the New Christian Right not only to help defeat candidates, but also to change the hearts and minds of legislators who were not Zionist. Jesse Helms represents a good example.

Until 1985, Senator Helms—one of Jerry Falwell's closest allies on all domestic issues, and it is said, a big financial supporter of Falwells's church—was known as one of the most vocal critics of the special relationship that exists between the U.S. and Israel. And especially of the large amounts of U.S. dollars that taxpayers send to Israel. Helms had always voted against foreign aid on principle and had a consistent record of blocking and attacking other initiatives important to Jews. His voting record was such that Israelis and friends of Israel termed him one of the most anti-Zionist if not the most anti-Zionist of all legislators.

The American-Israeli Jewish writer Sol Stern in an August 28, 1984, *Village Voice* article, gave this analysis: "Helms is the most reactionary senator of the past three decades and a fellow traveler of what some journalists have called the 'Fascist International.' He has publicly embraced Roberto D'Aubuisson, godfather of the El Salvador death squads and a charter member of the 'International' . . . Not surprisingly, Helms has the worst record of anyone in the Senate on aid to Israel. It's not even close. Some vote-counters at Jewish organizations record him as having vigorously opposed the last 26 bills favorable to Israel."

Helms also was outspoken about Israel's invasion of Lebanon, which resulted in the killing and wounding of more than 100,000 Lebanese and Palestinians. In a *Washington Post* interview, as a means of protest, he proposed the following remedy:

"Shut down relations (with Israel). Now, I know that will send a shudder to the (Israeli) lobby that's so powerful in this day. But shut off relations."

Then, rather suddenly, Helms made a 180-degree turn. He was on the Senate floor, and instead of criticizing Israel he was praising Israel. He was telling colleagues he had an invitation to visit the Jewish state and that he planned to go. Moreover, Helms signed his name to a letter addressed to President Reagan, in which he portrayed Israel as America's best ally in the Middle East and urged the President to help Israel retain the illegally occupied Arab territories of the West Bank, Gaza, the Golan Heights and Arab East Jerusalem.

What happened? For an opinion of the Helms' switch, I talked with Allan Kellum, editor of *MidEast Observer*, that reports on U.S. Congressional legislation as it relates to the Middle East. Could Kellum explain why the North Carolina senator had overnight become an avid Zionist? Was it Falwell who had changed the heart and mind of Senator Helms?

"They are good friends," Kellum, a former school teacher in the Middle East, began. "Both are ultra-conservatives. Both oppose abortion, a nuclear freeze, the Equal Rights Amendment and teaching an evolutionary development of the species. They also agree that all other creeds are inferior to theirs. And that unless one is born again in Christ, one does not have a religion that will take him or her to heaven.

"For years, Helms and Falwell were in total agreement on all major issues—except one. And that was Israel. In the 1970s and 1980s, Falwell moved more and more into the Zionist camp. He favored giving Israel any amount of money Israel wanted. And Helms was vehemently opposed to our doing so."

Had the Israeli lobby used its good friend Falwell to influence Helms?

"It probably did. Helms was re-elected even when he was against aid to Israel. But the Israelis may have used Falwell to tell Helms: 'Look, you saw what happened to Senator Percy. We defeated him. And if you do not change, you will not get elected the next time you run.' But as for those taking the actual credit for making Helms do the flip-flop, a conservative Israeli lobbying group, called Americans for a Safe Israel, did that," Kellum said.

I had heard of the main pro-Israeli lobby group—called American-Israel Public Affairs Committee or AIPAC. I knew it was in charge of dispensing the big money raised through PACs. But what was the main purpose of Americans for a Safe Israel?

"The purpose is to do to others, who are not pro-Zionists, what was done to Helms: to convince any conservative who has not been pro-Israel that in order to be elected or reelected he or she must support Israel—100 percent. AIPAC and the conservative Israeli lobby deal with different issues. AIPAC deals with aid and arms sales, while Americans for a Safe Israel has a neo-conservative agenda: it aims to convince Americans that Israel has an exclusive right to all of Jerusalem and all of Palestine."

In addition to aiding the Israeli lobby in Congress, the New Christian Right aids the Zionists in gaining greater access to the White House, Kellum said.

"I'm not saying that AIPAC's Thomas Dine or other Jewish leaders need Jerry Falwell to open doors for them in order to talk with the President. They don't. The friends of Israel have always found the doors open to every President beginning with Truman. But over the past years, as Israel and then the U.S. Jewish community and then the U.S. presidency turned more conservative, the Israelis realized it was expedient to become close to persons who were close to the president.

"And who has been closer to our last several presidents than Billy Graham? When President Reagan was shot, he asked first of all to see Billy Graham. Reagan chose two dispensationalist ministers, James Robison and W. A. Criswell, to give the opening and closing prayers at the Republican convention in Dallas. And he chose his California dispensationalist minister Donn Moomaw to give the benediction at his 1985 inauguration. Reagan felt comfortable with the dispensationalists. And if a Christian minister was not with the New Christian Right, Reagan did not see or talk with him.

"Now the evangelical-fundamentalist leaders have enormous political power," Kellum concluded. "The New Christian Right is the rising star of the Republican party. And Israel is reaping political benefits within the White House from its alliance with it."

What Israel Gains
from the Alliance

More Land

One evening on the 1985 Falwell tour, an Israeli guide named
Moses asked us to gather in a hotel auditorium. He wanted to explain Israel's wars of 1948, 1967, 1973 and 1982. He drew a map
and we sat listening to dates and places. Soon after he began his
personal odyssey in the ongoing conflict with Palestinians, Marvin,
the retired Kansas executive, who was seated near me rose and
without a word of explanation left the room.

The next morning, I sat next to Marvin on our tour bus. I asked
if he had left the guide's talk because he was tired. No, he said.
He did not need facts about Israel's wars. He knew in his heart "the
miracle of the Jews winning every war they've fought against the
Arabs. So I already know whose side I'm on—I'm on Israel's side."

Marvin and many others in the New Christian Right, I noted,
relish being allied with a winner. They identify with Old Testament
warriors who with swift swords and no mercy slew all their enemies.
Marvin liked the biblical texts that quoted a God opting for extreme
violence as divine policy. He once quoted to me Psalm 110 that
speaks of Yahweh crushing the heads and filling the earth with the
corpses of the non-believers, and Psalm 137 that expresses the wish
for vengeance by taking little Babylonian children and dashing them
against the rocks.

"This is the way the Israelis should treat the Arabs," Marvin said.

While Marvin was fascinated and could quote chapters and
verses from biblical history, he was not knowledgeable about today's Israeli-Arab conflict. And he was not interested in learning
because he already knew all that he felt God wanted him to know.
"Americans ought to learn from the Israelis how to fight wars,"
Marvin said.

Then did Marvin believe it was because of superior training that the Israelis had won so many of their wars against Palestinians and other Arabs?

"No, not really," he said. "It's because of God. Every war the Jewish soldiers fight is a battle directed by God Himself."

Marvin and most others on the Falwell-sponsored tours agreed that the Israelis should continually and by whatever means necessary make use of their military strength to expand the boundaries of Israel. The Jews, said Marvin, "are the only people in the world with divine rights to a land."

I recalled to Marvin a conversation I had in 1983 with Brad, the 35-year-old financial consultant. He had said we Christians were delaying the arrival of Christ by not helping the Jews take land from Palestinians. Did Marvin agree?

Yes, he said. Brad was right. "The Jews must own all of the land promised them by God before Christ can return. But it won't be long before the total redemption."

Redemption? I asked. I had grown up hearing this term and in the traditional Christian theological usage, I knew it applied to our deliverance from sin and our restoration to a communion with God—especially through Christ's sacrifice and divine forgiveness. Wasn't this, I asked Marvin, his definition of redemption?

"You are talking about a spiritual redemption," he said. "But before that can happen, God must deal with His nation, Israel. As now used in Israel, the term 'redemption' applies to Jewish National Fund acquisition of Gentile property in Greater Israel or 'Eretz Israel'—whether by legitimate purchase, forced sale, or outright expropriation."

His interpretation seemed far removed from what I had learned as a child. But Marvin held fast to the notion that his definition of "redemption"—meaning acquiring Arab lands—was the primary one.

In Washington, D.C., I learned that Christians, many of them in high government posts, pray around the clock to bring about the day that Palestinians will no longer be on their native land: it will belong exclusively to the Jews. I learned that Christians go to a half-million-dollar mansion in Washington, D.C., and that they direct their prayers not for all peoples everywhere, and not for peace on earth, and not for the poor, hungry, homeless or dispossessed. Rather, they pray for land—land now owned by Palestinians, which they want taken from them and placed into the hands of Israeli Jews.

Mrs. Bobi Hromas, wife of Dr. Leslie A. Hromas, a top official with a West Coast defense contractor, bought the mansion. She did so for one purpose: to provide a setting for Christians to pray for the "redemption" of land. Mrs. Hromas, who maintains other homes in suburban Los Angeles as well as Jerusalem, calls her organization the American Christian Trust. I first heard about her organization from Charles Fischbein, of Washington, D.C., who spent eleven years in Jewish communal work and was an executive director of the Jewish National Fund. One day Fischbein, who is in his 40s, agreed to a tape-recorded interview.

"In October of 1982, after three years as the executive director of the Jewish National Fund Middle Atlantic Region, Gideon Shamron, the Israeli Embassy's liaison with American Christians, called me. He wanted me to meet Bobi Hromas, founder and director of the American Christian Trust, which had just purchased an expensive residence in Northwest Washington," Fischbein began.

"I went to the residence and met Mrs. Hromas, who explained that the Trust was an umbrella agency for many of the major evangelical Christian movements, and that it acted as a conduit to send money directly to Israel.

"The Trust enjoys 501 (c)(3) status and receives funds from private individuals, estates and large evangelical-fundamentalists organizations. As part of my liaison work with her, I visited in the Hromas home in Rolling Hills, California. She also uses an office in Torrance and works with a group called En Agape (With Love) and receives funds from Hollywood celebrities, as well as from wealthy Texans, such as the Clint Murchisons, former owners of the Dallas Cowboys, and the Cowboys' football coach, Tom Landry, who does TV Bible commericals.

"The Trust in turn gives this money to Israel, expressly for Jewish settlements in the West Bank. The money is transmitted directly to the Embassy of Israel in Washington or carried to Israel by Mrs. Hromas, or it is transmitted through the Heritage International Bank in Bethesda, Maryland, which was founded by Donald

Wolpe, former president of the Zionist Organization of America and is the first and only bank in the United States that has branch banking in Israel.

"Mrs. Hromas told me the Trust planned to raise a hundred million dollars to purchase land for Jewish settlements in the West Bank, the present target area being in the Palestinian town of Hebron. She also said that tens of millions already have been given to the government of Israel, as well as for individual settlements in Hebron. This I was told would help fulfill biblical prophecy.

"Mrs. Hromas was very open about her connections with the major evangelical-fundamentalist preachers including Jerry Falwell, Pat Robertson, Jimmy Swaggart and others. She was also open about her connections with such long-time Reagan friends as Walter Annenberg, Edwin Meese, former Secretary of the Interior James Watt and Herb Ellingwood, a close Reagan friend and advisor for several decades.

"Shortly after my first meetings with Mrs. Hromas, she came to me saying that President Reagan and Herb Ellingwood wanted to plant a grove of trees in memory of Scott, son of the Edwin Meeses, who was killed in an automobile accident. Ellingwood wanted the trees planted in Hebron and Ed Meese agreed. I told Mrs. Hromas that because of the Jewish National Fund's tax-exempt status, we, that is, the Jewish National Fund, could not take money and channel it to the West Bank. She said she would go ahead and arrange through the Christian Embassy in Jerusalem to have trees planted in Hebron. And that she also would give the Jewish National Fund $5,000 to plant a grove of trees in Scott's name in Jerusalem."

Because of her many contributions to Israel, Israeli and American Zionists decided to honor Mrs. Hromas. "And they put me in charge of staging a dinner for her. She was one of the few—if not the only Gentile—to be so honored. And during the dinner, Herb Ellingwood presented Mrs. Hromas with a Bible signed by President Reagan."

In his visits to the American Christian Trust residence, had Fischbein, I asked, seen the chapel where Christians pray that Israelis take more Arab lands?

Yes, he said, Bobi Hromas had shown it to him. It was on the ground floor. "The residence is located at 39th and Reno Road, directly across from the Israeli embassy."

And did she deliberately choose a site facing the Israeli embassy? If so, for what purpose?

"Yes, she chose the location deliberately in order to be as close as possible to the embassy, and in turn, to the land where she directs her prayers—the land of Israel. She added the chapel after she bought the house. She designed it so if you are sitting there, praying for Israel, you can occasionally look out a large picture glass window to the Israeli embassy. The chapel has its own private door. And Mrs. Hromas invites members of Congress, the Senate, Joint Chiefs of Staff and even the President himself to partake in 24-hour-a-day prayer sessions for Israel. I was told that the Secret Service had requested that special glass be installed in the windows to protect the visitors inside the chapel," Fischbein said.

I knew the area. Reno Road traffic was heavy. Would not street noises interfere with one's prayers?

"No," he said. "The chapel is all soundproof. You don't hear a thing."

I wanted to visit, but I did not know how to arrange it. Fischbein, having become disillusioned with the Zionists' political goals, had broken ranks with them and would, for that reason, no longer be welcomed at the American Christian Trust.

Quite unexpectedly, however, I became a guest there. It happened like this: While on the 1985 Falwell tour, I dropped by the Christian Embassy in Jerusalem and visited with a personable young American employee named David. I liked him and invited him and his wife to lunch. We then drove in their car to Bethlehem. We enjoyed a pleasant lunch and drove back to Jerusalem. Knowing that I was returning in two days to Washington, he asked if I would hand carry a letter for him back to D.C.. The letter was to Mrs. Hromas at the American Christian Trust.

Back in Washington, I mailed the letter to Mrs. Hromas, then in California. Soon thereafter I received an invitation to a "high tea" at the residence of the Trust.

I attended, mingling with about 50 guests. I chatted with Richard and Mirian Hellman of Washington, D.C., who represent the Christian Embassy in Jerusalem; Rabbi and Mrs. Alex Pollack—he of Congregation Adas Israel; Carolyn Sundseth, associate director, the White House office of Public Liaison, and her husband, Victor Sundseth, representative of an evangelical fundamentalist mission in Maui, Hawaii; and Herb Ellingwood, who has said he often talked over the End of Time with Ronald Reagan when Reagan was governor. After Reagan became president, he named Ellingwood to head the Merit Protection Board.

At the high tea, I watched many guests shake Ellingwood's hand and congratulate him on placing fundamentalist Christians in high government posts. As I stood beside Ellingwood, both of us sipping tea, I listened to one guest after another speak to him in almost coded sentences: "I am aware of what you are doing . . . Praise the Lord!"

I also had an opportunity to chat awhile with Bobi Hromas, a strikingly attractive woman in her 50s, who stands about five feet, three inches and weighs about 115 pounds. She was dressed conservatively yet elegantly in a simple suit with a silk blouse. Her auburn hair was combed in a neat, short page-boy style. I was struck not only by her attractiveness, but also by her warmth and out-going personality. I learned she credits her great love for Israel to her mother, Dr. Pauline E. Parham of Dallas, a woman in her 70s, who travels the world as an Assemblies of God minister.

Some days later, Mrs. Edna Chupik, housekeeper for the Trust, a large, pleasant woman and a native Texan, called to ask me to take a "prayer vigil." I accepted. After I arrived at the residence, Mrs. Chupik played a 45-minute tape with the recorded voice of Mrs. Hromas explaining the necessity of getting land now in the hands of Palestinians into the hands of Jews, for otherwise—until the land is redeemed—we are delaying the Second Coming of Christ.

Mrs. Hromas' talk, taped in her California home, was an outpouring of anguished desire to be heard by God. "What is a watch?" she asked. "It is a petitioning of God. You are telling him, 'You can do something about this. And no one else can.' It is not sitting and meditating. That's not what it is. It is to give the Lord no rest, until He answers these prayers. That's praying. You will not be denied. He calls on us to take action, to do whatever has to be done. He calls on us for a commitment to do something about it. This makes you a global Christian, for the King of the earth . . .When you become a petitioner no negotiation with the enemy is possible . . ."

Not well organized, her talk was delivered with obvious deep and sincere emotion. At tape's end, I then walked alone to the chapel. I found a room with a coffee table and seven large beige velvet upholstered chairs. On the coffee table I found a copy of *The Living Bible* (in large print). the *Chronological Bible* and the *Holy Bible* (King James Version). I also saw a notebook containing the names of our government officials, beginning with President Reagan, as well as a list of the officials in Israel, including the names of all members of the Israeli parliament.

I looked out the large picture window to the busy Reno Road traffic. Fischbein was right, I was not disturbed by noise. From my vantage point, I could see not only the Israeli embassy, but also in the distance the Jordanian embassy. Interestingly, they have similar architecture, both being four stories high and constructed of similar beige-colored stones.

Since I was there to pray, I composed a number of prayers. And since each prayer watch last three hours, I took the time to write my prayers in my notebook. They do not bear repeating, but they were prayers not only for the leaders of America and Israel but for all peoples—so vulnerable to having their lives blotted out in a nuclear Armageddon, which could so easily be triggered over the confiscation of Palestinian lands.

After three hours, Edna Chupik descended the steps to remind me my watch was up, "unless you want to stay longer." I got my coat, and she accompanied me outside to Reno Road, where she helped me flag a taxi. En route home, I pondered anew the mission of Bobi Hromas: to get money to Israel to purchase Palestinian lands (or supply money to Jewish settlers who take the land at gun point).

As always, attempting to understand the belief system of the dispensationalists, I felt sad. Instead of "redeeming" land halfway around the world, I wondered why a Christian could not help and comfort those who are oppressed—as did Christ—all within the radius of a few miles. I could not think of a single instance in which Christ urged his followers to "redeem" land. His kingdom, he said, was within.

Nevertheless, dispensationalists see it otherwise: they give money to Israelis to help them take land from Palestinians by whatever means available. Land fraud is one of these.

A huge land scandal was made public August 6, 1985, when police arrested three Israeli men suspected of forging documents related to illegal purchases of thousands of acres of Arab lands in the West Bank. The men, well-known personalities with extensive military and government connections, were accused of being paid over two million U.S. dollars to take land by fraudulent means from Palestinians. It is possible that a portion of that money came from right-wing Christians who are convinced their highest Christian hopes lie in the Jews taking possession of all Palestinian land.

An Israeli Justice Ministry official said as much as $100 million may have changed hands for thousands of acres of Arab-owned property that was taken through forgery, deceit, intimidation and, occasionally, force.

Two members of the Israeli parliament, Yossi Sarid and Dudi Zucker in a letter to the Minister of Police said "there are suspicions of fraud in colossal proportions," and they added the fraudulent land deals took place "under the auspices of government institutions."

Threats by three arrested Israelis to reveal the names of top officials sent shock waves through the right-wing Likud bloc, which had initiated the bogus land-buying scheme. One Israeli who headed the Israeli Land Administration resigned, while others promptly either disassociated themselves from the scandal or tried to soften its effect on the public.

On August 19, 1985, Likud leader and Foreign Minister Yitzhak Shamir warned Israelis not to take the matter too seriously. "Do not touch the issue of land redemption," he said. "Sometimes tricks and schemes are needed and unconventional means used to purchase and redeem land. It is intolerable that the investigation of isolated cases of land purchases should turn into a general witch-hunt on all land purchases (in occupied Palestine), with the aim of preventing the Zionist mission."

The mission of political, militant Zionism has been to take all the land of the Palestinians.

In 1918, the Palestinians represented about 90 percent of the population and they owned about 98 percent of the land, the Jews having only two percent of the land.

In 1947, the Palestinians owned about 93.96 of the land and the Jews only 6.04 percent. In that year the U.N. voted to partition Palestine—allocating one half of Palestine to the Jews and the other half for Palestinians. In a statement to the United Nations Special Committee on Palestine, Moshe Shertok, at that time head of the political Department of the Jewish Agency, said, "Today, we possess just over six percent of the land area of Palestine."

In its 1967 war, Israel seized large segments of Arab land and has since refused to abide by international law stating land seized by military conquest may not legally be held. By early 1986 Israel had its soldiers in more than one-half of the portion of Palestine promised by the U.N. resolution to the Arabs. Only about 20 percent of Mandate Palestine was still in the hands of the indigenous Palestinians.

Christian zealots such as Marvin and Bobi Hromas were convinced—and I believe sincerely—that they should help Israel dispossess the Palestinians of what little they had left. As Marvin had put it, the Jews had "historic rights" to the land.

H. G. Wells, English writer and popular historian, said in this connection, "If it is proper to 'reconstitute' a Jewish state which has not existed for 2,000 years, why not go back another thousand years, and reconstitute the Canaanite state?" The Canaanites, unlike the Jews, continued to be there all through history.

As far as "historic rights go," if the world is to be run exclusively according to rules set or declared by those who say they possess such rights, Moors who were in Spain for 700 years could declare they have "historic rights" to the land and ask the Spaniards to get out. And the Indians who were in America for thousands of years before it was "discovered" by white Europeans could say to non-Indians living in America today: we have "historic rights" so you get out. There has to be a point of departure, a time when we live not as Jewish settlers in occupied Palestine—by force of Uzi machine guns—but rather by community, state and international laws.

Where Israel is concerned, the 1947 U.N. resolution represents the point of departure to which might be added the agreements made under U.N. auspices concerning the armistice borders of 1929.

All world leaders have upheld the validity of the U.N. resolution that called for Palestine to provide land for both Jewish immigrants and native Palestinians. In addition, many of the world's foremost Jewish leaders, including Bruno Kreisky, former prime minister of Austria, and Philip M. Klutznick of Chicago, president emeritus of the World Jewish Congress, deny that Jews have the right to retain territories taken in conquest after Israel became a state. They point out that in a secular sense, for Jews to claim they have a "historic right" to land beyond its U.N. created borders means a regression back to the days of "manifest destiny"—a 19th-century policy of imperialist expansion. Today, they stress, we are attempting to live in a 20th-century atmosphere of anti-colonialism and respect for human rights.

Several million American Christians however believe man-made laws do not apply, and they are intent on the Jews' confiscating, and thereby "redeeming" all the land of Palestine. If this brings on World War III, and a nuclear Armageddon, they will think they have done God's will.

What Israel Gains from the Alliance

Christian Grassroots Support

Evangelical-fundamentalist lay leader Krieger, in an analysis paper prepared for Israeli and American Jewish leaders, lists 250 pro-Israel evangelical organizations "of varying size and depth in America."

"Most have developed during the past five years"—that is, in the 1980s—, Kreiger reports, adding that the groups specialize in events such as "Solidarity Rallies for Israel" or "Israel Awareness Gatherings" in Protestant churches. "Still others are into touring, publication ministries, prophetical conferences, theological support, etc. A few groups venture into direct political support in various lobbying efforts by direct letter writing campaigns and/or media-oriented events which have a strong pro-Israel expression associated with them."

Zionists, working in alliance with evangelical-fundamentalists, created—to name only a very few of the 250 support groups—these organizations:

— The National Christian Leadership Conference for Israel (NCLCI). Franklin H. Littell, a Christian Zionist and a professor at Temple University in Pennsylvania, was named president. Dr. Littell, a Methodist, who is perhaps the most vocal of all Christian supporters of Israel, told me in a personal interview that "to be Christian is to be Jewish," and that it was the duty of a Christian to put support of the "land of Israel" above all else. He bases his love for Israel not on the dispensationalists' belief system, but rather on what he perceives to be a Christian necessity to atone for the suffering of Jews in the Nazi holocaust.

To rally support for Israel's armed attack on Lebanon, the National Christian Leadership Conference for Israel in 1982 ran a full-page *Washington Post* and *New York Times* advertisement entitled, "Christians in Solidarity with Israel." The Christians stated:

"Our solidarity with the Jewish people and the State of Israel is part of a commitment to peace and justice for all people in the Middle East. We believe it is the basic right and duty of every government to ensure the safety and security of its citizens." The ad did not mention concern for those of Christian or Muslim faiths who live in the Middle East. The Christians signing the ad said they fully supported the Israeli invasion of Lebanon, and they further indicated those who opposed Israel's policies were anti-Semitic.

Issac C. Rottenberg, a Jew who converted to Dutch Reformed Protestantism, served as executive director of this organization, which is closely linked to the International Christian Embassy in Jerusalem and includes among its staunchest supporters such dispensationalist ministers as W. A.Criswell, Jim Bakker and Pat Robertson.

— The National Christian Congress (NCC), which was spawned by the above mentioned organization, NCLCI, was formed prior to the U.S. House of Representatives' vote on the sale of radar system aircraft (AWACS) to Saudi Arabia.

Professor Littell, who said the NCC was formed to unite Christians from a diversity of denominations and organizations in their common concern for the safety of the Jewish homeland, further stated that the proposed sale of aircraft to Saudi Arabia represented "the most crucial time on the calendar for Israel's survival." The NCC dutifully voiced its strong objection to the proposed AWACS sale.

At the initial NCC meeting, which attracted about 100 participants including not only fundamentalists but also representatives of the National Conference of Catholic Bishops and the National Council of Churches, New York Republican Representative Jack Kemp called the establishment of Israel in 1948 "a fulfillment of biblical prophecy." He said he thought of himself as "a serious Bible student" and added that the role of the United States is "to preserve opportunities (in Israel) for biblical prophecies to come true."

— Christians United For American Security. This organization seems to have been created for one purpose: to produce names as sponsors for full-page ads opposing defensive weaponry for Saudi

Arabia. Dozens of Christian Zionists signed the ad, including Jerry Falwell and a Roman Catholic nun who is president of Manhattan-ville College.

— TAV Evangelical Ministries, named for the last letter of the Hebrew alphabet. In 1982, during the Israeli invasion of Lebanon, the Zionists used TAV to arrange several West Coast conferences of evangelical-fundamentalists with Jewish leaders. And in November of that year TAV sponsored a "Solidarity Sabbath" at the Washington Hebrew Congregation. This synagogue's senior rabbi, Joshua O. Haberman, acted as host. A number of rabbis attended, as did the chairman of the board of the Zionist Organization of America and a representative of the Israeli lobby, the American Israeli Public Affairs Committee (AIPAC), which might have picked up the tab for bringing about 1,500 fundamentalists and Jewish leaders to the nation's capital in order that they might formally—and with *Washington Post* newspaper coverage—endorse Israel's invasion of Lebanon.

Dr. John Walvoord, president of the Dallas Theological Seminary, told me he was one of the speakers at this affair. He said, "I talked to the gathering about God's promise to the nation of Israel—and they loved it."

— The American Coalition for Traditional Values (ACTV). Spearheaded by San Diego preacher and popular writer Tim LeHaye, an avowed pro-Israel dispensationalist, ACTV is the grass-roots political organizing arm of the Religious Right. The group's purpose, according to its propaganda brochure, is to politically manipulate 45 million fundamentalists through "an aggressive voter registration drive and election day get-out-the-vote campaign" and to get fundamentalists into government service "through our talent bank." Leaders in this organization include Falwell, Swaggart, Jim Bakker and Pat Robertson.

— The Christian Voice, based in California, with a lobbying office in Washington, D.C., claims 190,000 members, including 37,000 ministers. It has an estimated yearly budget of $1.5 million. Its political action arm, Christian Voice Moral Government Fund, formed an avowedly partisan campaign operation entitled "Christians for Reagan."

Krieger names as "leading lights" among strongly pro-Israel

evangelical-fundamentalists Ed McAteer of the Religious Round Table, which sponsors an annual Prayer Breakfast for Israel; Ben Armstrong, executive director of the National Religious Broadcasters; Adrian Rogers, senior pastor of Bellevue Baptist Church in Memphis and former president of the Southern Baptist Convention; and W. A. Criswell, senior minister of the First Baptist Church of Dallas.

Like Rogers, Criswell is a former president of the Southern Baptist Convention. They are two of the leading right-wing leaders of the convention committed to purging liberals, neo-orthodox and other non-evangelicals, non-dispensationalists from Southern Baptist institutions and agencies. Criswell, like Falwell, is totally committed to a militarily strong Israel. He has maintained close ties with Israeli right-wing leaders, and especially with former Prime Minister Begin.

Jer USA lem

Mixing Politics
and Religion

To whom does Jerusalem belong? Is it only a piece of real estate, the pawn of those with the biggest army and weapons? Or, as the United Nations declared, when it carved a homeland out of Palestine for the Jews, is it to be a city for three faiths—Christians, Muslims and Jews, with the framework for its government decided by the big powers under international law?

The Israelis demand exclusive ownership of the city holy to about a billion Christians, almost a billion Muslims and about 14 million Jews. To make their claim, that they legitimately own the City of Three Faiths, the Israelis—a majority of whom do not believe in God—say that God wanted the Hebrews and/or Jews to have Jerusalem in perpetuity. To mount a public relations campaign with this message, the Israelis turned to Mike Evans, a Jewish American who was not generally known to the American public or for that matter even to many of the evangelical-fundamentalist-charismatic branch of Christianity, to which he had converted.

I first learned about Mike Evans' Israeli promotional campaign when I saw a Fort Worth *Star-Telegram* ad promoting a "live, via satellite from Jerusalem" performance with "Mike Evans, Jewish evangelist." I was at this time visiting in Fort Worth with my mother Mrs. H. H. (Ruth) Halsell and sister Margaret Parker. I showed them the ad and we decided to attend.

With Margaret driving, we left Mother's home on October 20, 1984 and drove past the impressive Bass Brothers skyscrapers, toward Meadowbrook. Leaving the turnpike, we entered pecan-shaded Oakland and continuing for another ten miles, we arrived at a large, modern structure without windows called Bethel Temple.

As we entered the church, we were greeted by an usher who handed us a program:

Jer USA lem, D.C. an Historic Event,
October 20, 1984. Live via Satellite
from Jerusalem, Israel, David's Capital.

We proceeded down an aisle, while members of the congregation were standing and singing—many with arms raised over their
heads, which they moved in a rhythm backward and forward. We
took our places in the second row from the front and listened to
a few opening words from the church pastor, John M. Wilkerson.
In his mid-50s and of medium height, with dark reddish hair, he
wore a well-tailored suit and aviator type glasses.

We looked beyond the pastor to a large screen, and to two men,
both wearing business suits and holding pliers in their hands. We
all riveted our eyes on them rather than on Brother Wilkerson, who
continued talking, at one point saying, "I hope I'm not boring you."
The men with pliers took a cursory look at the TV screen and
walked offstage. Then they reentered with a roll of wire as large
as a bushel basket and pretended to attach this wire to the screen.

"They have been working on the set all day," said Pastor Wilkerson, in a statement that strained credulity. The workmen seemed
as much a part of the props as the screen itself, obviously placed
on stage to give some faint credence to the ad promoting a program "direct via satellite from Jerusalem." While our curiosity and
confusion grew, a woman in the audience raised her voice and asked
Pastor Wilkerson a simple question:

"Please tell us, what is this all about? Who is Mike Evans?"

Taking his cue, Pastor Wilkerson launched into a long story in
which he told us that those who wanted to get to the "Biggies"
should stick with "good ol' Mike." By way of example Wilkerson
told this story:

"I got an invitation to the Republican convention and I didn't
want to go alone, so I called Mike Evans and said, 'Could I go with
you?' And Mike says, 'Well of course.' When we went there and
got to a door, there was the football star Rosey Grier who is just
gigantic, you know. He knows good ol' Mike, and he says, 'You just
follow me.' So we follow Rosey—his back is about four feet wide,
and he's pushing his way through that crowd—and he leads us
right up to where the Biggies are, and there we are standing by

George Bush!

"We are right up there with the Biggies! And suddenly someone is introducing Mike Evans and saying this is the Reverend Mike Evans. Evans waves to the crowd, and then suddenly someone is introducing me! This is the Reverend John Wilkerson and I am waving to the crowd—just as if I were somebody, just as if I were one of those politicians, one of the Biggies."

Pastor Wilkerson had made his point: Mike Evans is Somebody and important persons such as George Bush know him. People will make a path for him in the circles that count. "He is moving in Republican circles and getting people to vote—for our kind of people, Reagan and Bush," Pastor Wilkerson said. "He believes in an America that supports Israel. Because he believes in strength, he believes in an America that supports our only safe, reliable ally in the Middle East—the only democracy over there, Israel!"

Then Pastor Wilkerson went on to explain that "Mike Evans is of the Jewish faith. And he converted to Christianity to help his people, but this doesn't mean he goes to Israel and tries to convert Jews. Oh, nothing of that sort of thing. But he wants to show Israel and the Jews we love them, that we stand by them, and to impress upon them by our presence—and our gifts—our great love. No one in all the world has suffered as much as the Jews. And God tells us that He is going to bless those who bless the Jews."

After we had all sat waiting about an hour, Wilkerson said, "Obviously the big screen is not going to work," whereupon the two walk-on actors rolled out a 22-inch screen TV set and those in the side pews moved to center, and we soon were viewing Mike Evans—not live via satellite but engaging enough, and holding a Bible in his right hand, which to punctuate his points, he effectively thrust toward his listeners.

Mustachioed, with jet black hair slicked down and parted on a slant, and attired in a sapphire blue suit, Evans exuded charismatic charm and unbounded natural energy. He began talking in an almost endless stream:

"I am standing on the Mount of Olives, overlooking the City of Jerusalem, David's capital," he announced. I noted that on the screen Al Aqsa Mosque dominated the background—as it has dominated the historic city of Jerusalem for 700 years.

For an hour Evans frequently repeated himself, saying God wanted Americans to move their embassy from Tel Aviv to Jerusalem because "Jerusalem is David's Capital and Satan is attempting to prevent the Jews from having the right to choose their capital.

"It will cost the lives of your own sons and fathers if you do not recognize Jerusalem as Jewish property. God will bless those who bless Israel and curse those who curse Israel."

We saw a supporting cast of TV evangelists—Pat Robertson, Jerry Falwell, Jimmy Swaggart, as well as singer Pat Boone, author Hal Lindsey, and columnist Jack Anderson. Additionally, we saw film clips of Evans in Jewish skullcap talking to the chief rabbi of Israel—both nodding in agreement that "Jerusalem belongs exclusively to the Jews."

Throughout the program Mike Evans repeatedly asked listeners to "Write out your check and do it now. Write it for 'Jerusalem D.C.' If you think you can give only $25, make it $50. And if you think you can give only $50, make it $100. And if you can give only $100, make it $1,000!"

Mother, Margaret and I looked in front of us and we glanced in back of us and to the left and to the right, and in every direction we saw men and women writing checks. Before dismissing the congregation, Pastor Wilkerson asked everyone in the audience to sign a petition to move the U.S. embassy to Jerusalem. As far as we could ascertain, most everyone did.

On another day, I took a 15-minute drive from Fort Worth to the suburban town of Bedford, Texas, which Evans says is his home. I talked with the mayor, who said he had never seen Evans. I visited the Chamber of Commerce and was told they did not know Evans and he was not in their listing of Bedford churches or ministries. I talked with several long-time residents and none had ever seen Evans. While one might expect a Christian minister who lists Bedford as his address to have a church, home or office there, Evans has none of these. He uses it merely for a P.O. box number.

I then secured a tape cassette of an hour-long television special Evans made in 1983 called "Israel, America's Key to Survival." In this film, Evans uses the word "crucial" to describe the role played by Israel in the political fate of the United States. Despite the fact that the film has a conspicuous political thrust, Evans and his Zionist sponsors, by labeling it as "religious programming," have secured free broadcast time on local television stations in at least 25 states, in addition to the Christian Broadcast Network cable system.

In this film, Evans makes a number of sensationalized political assertions about the importance of Israel to the United States, contending that if Israel were to relinquish territories that it illegally occupied, God Himself would destroy both Israel and the United States. Evans concludes his film with an appeal for Christians to come to the support of "America's best friend in that part of the world" by signing a "Proclamation of Blessing for Israel."

Between October 1984 and April 1985, Evans' one-hour television special, "Jerusalem, D.C." aired on 250 television stations. Later it was revised, making use of professional actors and aired again during the summer of 1985, with the apparent intent of softening American taxpayers for Israel's gargantuan aid request to the U.S. Congress as well as to gather support for the Zionist goal to persuade the U.S. to move its embassy from Tel Aviv to Jerusalem.

Since I learned nothing about Evans in my visit to Bedford, I wrote to his P.O. box address, and in return his computer responded with a series of letters, addressing me variously as "Beloved," "Partner," and "Lover of Israel." Evans' messages arrive in a variety of sizes and shapes including through-the-mail telegrams marked "personal and confidential." In one letter Evans writes:

"When I was four, a precious saint of the Lord knocked on our door. My mother had seven children, and even though she came from an Orthodox Jewish background, when this Christian lady asked her if she could take the children to Vacation Bible School, my mother gladly said 'Yes,' thinking it wouldn't do us any harm. Little did she know that Mrs. Zignoni would love us, share Scripture with us, plant the seeds that would eventually bring me into the Kingdom of God.

"What a joy it was to fly back to Springfield, Massachusetts, almost fifteen years after being in the ministry, having traveled two and one-half million miles, to hug Mrs. Zignoni and thank her for her labor of love . . ."

Evans also writes that he was a "37-year-old evangelist" and

"Jewish person" whom God had "divinely called and anointed . . ." He signs his letters with his name, followed by "Under Divine Appointment."

In a small pamphlet called "Partners in Prophecy '85," which features a cover photo of Evans and wife, Carolyn, praying in front of a Jewish menorah, he writes:

"More than 2,000 people responded to the altar call, but the most amazing thing was that as we went into the counseling tent, the convicting power of the Holy Spirit fell into a mighty roar. The weeping and travailing was so strong that I had to wait for over one hour to even talk.

"As I stood in amazement, 200 homosexuals came to the front, crying and repenting and praying for deliverance." Mysteriously Evans does not give the details of when and where this event took place. We are left with a lot of questions, such as, how did he know his converts were all homosexuals? His own eyes, Evans tells us, were "as big as saucers" as he " beheld Father God destroying the works of the devil and setting the captives free."

In another message, Evans says: "I close with our Lord's last words in Revelation 22:20. 'Surely, I come quickly.' Let's stand up and be counted in our belief that Jerusalem is the rightful capital of Israel."

In one letter was a photo of a smiling Evans with General Ariel Sharon, the mastermind of Israel's 1982 invasion of Lebanon, who met with the evangelist in Jerusalem "to discuss the military situation in Israel, and to express his (Sharon's) appreciation for the prayers and love of Christians." Clearly, preachers such as Evans love power— *cosmic* power—and close connections with Israel give them a feeling of power and influence on an international level.

Evans also enclosed a photo of himself with Jerusalem Mayor Teddy Kollek and with then Prime Minister Shamir, as well as a photo of tall Mike Evans towering over President Reagan. In still another letter, Evans tells about a 1983 visit to the White House. "Little did I know that the President of the United States would invite me to the White House or that God would stand me up to challenge 58 generals and admirals with the truth of God in the middle of a White House meeting . . . or little did I know a speech written by me calling America to stand by Israel would be put into the Congressional Record."

A year later Evans is again in the White House: "In 1984 the President invited approximately 90 of the most influential evangelical leaders to the White House to meet with some of the top Jewish rabbis and Jewish leaders in the world.

"As I sat in the east wing of the White House next to my good friend Jimmy Swaggart, Robert McFarlane, National Security Advisor, told us that United States foreign policy could not be determined by the Bible and that Jerusalem was not Israel's capital. He further stated that the status of Jerusalem had to be determined by negotiation with the Arab world.

"I turned to Jimmy Swaggart and said, 'Jimmy are you going to do anything about that statement?' He said, 'Mike, God has anointed you in behalf of Israel and you should stand and speak.'

"I stood and told Mr. McFarlane that the Bible was non-negotiable and God would not bless America if we turned our back on His Holy Word. I further stated that evangelical Christians would under no condition turn their backs on the Jewish people or the Word of God.

"Everyone started applauding, including about 40 of the most powerful rabbis in America."

Then in January, 1985, Evans says, "President Reagan invited Jim Bakker, Jimmy Swaggart, Jerry Falwell, myself and a few others to meet with him in private. I will never forget what he told us. The President expressed the belief that America was on the verge of a spiritual awakening. And I believe it with all my heart. God is raising up people like you and me in intercessory prayer and love to prepare the world for the return of the King of Kings and Lord of Lords."

In Israel, Evans says he has met with Labor's Prime Minister Shimon Peres as well as the Likud leaders. "I have met virtually all of the major leaders in the nation of Israel including eleven meetings with former Prime Minister Begin and other top government officials . . . I have been meeting with the Israeli Prime Minister and other top government officials on a regular basis." Evans adds he has a close association with Dr. Reuben Hecht of the prime minister's office, Dr. Benzion Netanyahu, president of the Jonathan Institute on world terrorism and Isser Harel, former head of the Israeli intelligence and security.

Israelis told him about their plan to invade Lebanon "two days before it occurred," Evans says. "I prayed with (Prime Minister) Begin for 24 hours immediately prior to the 1982 invasion of Lebanon," he writes.

In all of his letters, Evans reminds us that the Israelis see him as a special friend. During the time he was in Jerusalem filming "Jerusalem, D.C." Evans says an ultra-orthodox rabbi—Evans does not tell his name—laid his hands on his head and "prayed for me. Such a rabbi never lays his hands upon a Christian's head and prays or allows a Christian to lay their hands on his head and pray, but (for me) he prayed the prayer that only a Levite (priest) would pray in the Holy of Holies."

Because many Israeli leaders consider him close to them, they invited him to show "Jerusalem, D.C." on the government-owned television network. Before his appearance, Evans says, the Israelis had never permitted any Christian minister—not even friends like Billy Graham or Jerry Falwell—to appear on Israeli TV. There is an Israeli law forbidding a Christian to speak to a Jew or a gathering of Jews about Christ. But the Israelis knew Evans' message was political from the start. Evans explains his invitation to appear on Israeli TV:

"The Director General of Israeli Government Television Network was so impressed after watching 'Jerusalem, D.C.' that he invited me to fly to Israel and be on Israeli television as their guest and then show 'Jerusalem, D.C.' to the entire nation of Israel. It will be the first time in the history of the nation of Israel that a Christian has been on the government television network."

Evans then invited American Jews to watch his TV special, and he "rejoiced knowing that over 150,000 Jewish people in America alone saw this special, and we received over 14,500 calls from Jewish people." Evans wrote to all American synagogues, offering to send "absolutely free" a videocassette of "Jerusalem, D.C." Evans said many rabbis praised the film.

"My first thought at the conclusion of the videotape was 'Praise the Lord and pass the ammunition!' " wrote J. Rothmann, president of the Zionist Organization of America. "Your work is a hymn of praise and 'Jerusalem D.C.' is the very best ammunition. David's

capital is the capital of Israel and your outstanding video states the
case clearly and precisely. I hope that 'Jerusalem D.C.' is seen and
supported by millions."

Evans wants a million Christians to sign a petition such as the
one distributed in the Fort Worth church service I attended. Evans
writes: "I need your help in enlisting one million people or more
who will sign the International Petition to recognize Jerusalem as
the Rightful Capital of Israel.

"This is a spiritual petition that I will personally deliver to our
President, the Prime Minister of Israel and heads of states of other
nations. I've asked the Lord to move upon the hearts of at least
one million people to sign this historic petition. And I want YOU
to sign this much-needed and historic Petition immediately and rush
it back to me."

In 1984, Evans collected two volumes of signatures, hand carried
the names to Israel, and presented them to Prime Minister Shamir,
a hardened fighter and former terror-squad leader.

"Tears filled the prime minister's eyes and he said, 'Mike, these
Christians really do love us, don't they?' " Evans writes.

"I said, 'Yes they do, Prime Minister, they really love you, they
really care.' And then the Prime Minister said, 'These are *real* people, aren't they?' " Evans then continues his form letter, "Beloved,
Israel is shocked that people like you and me would share such
grace, love and compassion with them."

In yet another letter Evans says, "Our government is guilty of
not vetoing an anti-Israel resolution in the United Nations Security Council which called all members to withdraw their embassies
from that city on the grounds Jerusalem was not part of 'Arab territories occupied by Israel.' In consequence, 13 nations that had
established embassies in Jerusalem as Israel's capital withdrew.

"The Bible says that God Almighty declared Jerusalem as Israel's
capital in the time of King David, when He told Solomon to build
the temple there; and that we are to pray for the peace of Jerusalem,
that it might prosper. (Psalm 122:6)

"Nevertheless, America refuses to recognize Jerusalem. Our nation considers Jerusalem an occupied territory, but not Israel's
capital. For over three decades, the United States has refused to
recognize Israel's sovereignty over any part of the city, that is why

the American embassy is located in Tel Aviv!

"America is calling for the redivision of Jerusalem. Furthermore, the Ambassador of the American Embassy in Tel Aviv has no official role or status in Jerusalem. He can't even stamp a U.S. visa in Jerusalem! Why doesn't America recognize Jerusalem? Because we say that Jordan at one time controlled part of Jerusalem. That is true. But they controlled it illegally.

"Israel was promised that capital biblically; it was given those territories back historically by the British," Evans concludes.

It is true that Jordan prior to 1967, for a brief period, had control over Jerusalem, just as the British did before the Jordanians and the Turks before the British, and so on for the past 2,000 years.

The truth that Mike Evans overlooks, however, is that the Old City of Jerusalem is predominantly inhabited by Palestinian Christians and Palestinian Muslims today and that Palestinians and their forebears have lived and been the overwhelmingly vast majority of inhabitants for at least 2,000 years.

In 1980, Prime Minister Begin illegally annexed Arab Jerusalem, an action denounced by all world leaders. No major world government has recognized Israel's exclusive right to the City of Three Faiths, and no major government keeps its embassy in Jerusalem. If the United States made this move, it would be the first and only major world government to give legitimacy to Israel's exclusive claim to the City of Three Faiths. (Only one or two Central American countries, beholden to Israel for weapons, have opened embassies in Jerusalem since all embassies left in 1980 in protest to Begin's illegal annexation of the city.)

In 1947, when the United Nations Resolution recommended dividing Palestine into a Jewish country and a Palestinian country, neither side was to have Jerusalem. Indeed the U.N. partition resolution of November 29, 1947, expressly *excluded* Jerusalem from the settlement ("corpus separatum" was the language the U.N. used) and expressly stated that this "corpus separatum" would, when it was set up, be under international sovereignty. In short Jerusalem was to be neither a Jewish city nor a Christian or a Muslim Palestinian city, and for 39 years, from 1947 to 1986, world leaders insisted there be no change in this status until all parties to the conflict resolved the issue of the City of Three Faiths.

Epilogue

There is a scriptural text that states, "I have set before you life and death, blessing and cursing: therefore choose life, that both thou and thy seed may live." (Deuteronomy 30:19) I have thought about our choice of life or death over the past several years, listening to Jerry Falwell and other evangelists who come to us across the dial. Bible in hand and quoting from the Old Testament Book of Daniel and the New Testament Book of Revelation, they say God has foreordained that we must fight a nuclear war with Russia.

Convinced that a nuclear Armageddon is an inevitable event within the divine scheme of things, many evangelical dispensationalists have committed themselves to a course for Israel that, by their own admission, will lead directly to a holocaust indescribably more savage and widespread than any vision of carnage that could have generated in Adolph Hitler's criminal mind.

I have found their sermons thought provoking and shocking in their urging us to prepare for the End of the World. They cause me to realize that we have come a long distance from our beginnings as human beings. Most of us hold as the highest mark of civilized life being good neighbors: treating others as we would like them to treat us. And beyond that, so many have lived with an even more noble goal: to leave this world a better place than they found it.

The dispensationalists' sermons make me realize anew that I and billions of human beings before me have been lucky. We have been able to come into this world and, as our brightest hope, to look forward to a better tomorrow. Now for the first time in all of history, we have the ability to destroy all of cultural and human existence, eliminating not only all of those who are living today but all the future, all the tomorrows.

Sometimes I walk in a park and see the magic of a tree chang-

195

ing its wardrobe from winter to spring, or I listen to Mozart, read Shakespeare or see the miracle of a child's small hand so delicately and perfectly designed, and I think: how is it possible that we, with our own free will, are thinking seriously of choosing to destroy all of this miracle of life?

In his widely discussed book, *The Fate of the Earth*, Johathan Schell says it is important to make a clear distinction between the suffering and deaths of billions of persons, on the one hand, and the further almost ungraspable issue of the obliteration of the entire human future, on the other.

"The possibility that the living can stop the future generations from entering into life compels us to ask basic new questions about our existence, the most sweeping of which is what these unborn ones mean to us. No one has ever thought to ask this question before our time, because no generation before ours has ever held the life and death of the species in its hands . . . how are we to comprehend the life or death of the infinite number of possible people who do not yet exist at all?

"How are we, who are part of human life, to step back from life and see it whole, in order to assess the meaning of its disappearance?" Schell asks. "Death cuts off life; extinction cuts off birth. Death dispatches into the nothingness after life each person who has been born; extinction in one stroke locks up in the nothingness before life all the people who have not yet been born . . .

"The threat of the loss of birth . . . assails everything that people hold in common, for it is the ability of our species to produce new generations which assures the continuation of the world in which all our common enterprises occur and have their meaning."

In addition to reading Schell, I have followed the scientific findings of physicists, astronomers and others who warn that if either of the big powers should unleash nuclear weapons, dust from the explosions and resulting fires will pervade the entire planet earth. No one in any corner of the world, not in New Zealand or Tierra del Fuego, will escape the darkened masses of dust that will prevent the sun's rays from reaching earth, resulting in a nuclear winter that kills all plant and animal life.

In listening to Falwell preach and in reading Schell and Carl Sagan, I find they are looking at our possible extinction of all future tomorrows from two different viewpoints. I have heard Falwell preach on a nuclear Armageddon, and I saw his face turn radiant at the thought.

I find a vast difference between the fundamentalism of my childhood and the fundamentalism of today. In my childhood, preachers often denounced movies, dancing, whisky and evolution. Brother Turner and even J. Frank Norris had only limited funds and they did not have television and there was no state of Israel—that is, no official site for an Armageddon. Most important, there was no atomic bomb. Today Falwell, Pat Robertson and other dispensationalists seemingly have unlimited financial resources. They have a battle site in Israel and a line of reasoning for a nuclear war—God wills it. And they preach, promote and actually sell Americans on the idea of building more bombs and then using them.

The preachers in my childhood, advancing their belief in the Virgin Birth of Christ and God's creation in six days of the universe, were dealing with events of the past. And thus they presented no menace to our existence. Like apocalyptic Marxists, Falwell and other fundamentalists today have embraced a cult of *their* scenario of our future. And since the dispensationalists say our future lies in war and annihilation, they pose a danger entirely different and more far-reaching than that of the earlier evangelicals and fundamentalists.

I have attempted to show that the Israeli-U.S. fundamentalist alliance is not a confluence of theological doctrine or spiritual beliefs. Rather it is a working partnership founded on factors that are more political and military than theological. This cannot be otherwise because the religious emphases that characterize the Jewish state are based on strains of Judaism that regard Christian proselytizing—a basic premise of fundamentalists—as a profound threat to the existence of Jews as a community.

Despite the fact that in a religious sense the Christian fundamentalists and the political leaders of Israel are worlds apart, they are currently on good terms. We need not, however, believe that they are best of friends even though each side goes out of its way to assure us that they are.

We know that because the partners in the alliance have different long-term goals, their alliance and working arrangement must necessarily remain temporary. Nevertheless, despite being temporary, it can last long enough to cause a catastrophe of far-reaching consequences. If we do not recognize the danger they pose, the extremists will have time enough in their unsacred alliance to trigger a war that would not end until we have destroyed Planet Earth through self-fulfilling prophecy.

The United States and Russia, along with West Germany, England and France have made the Middle East the focal point in the arms race, reports the Middle East Council of Churches, which represents some 10 million Christians in the Middle East. The Council in its April-May 1984 *Perspectives* magazine, adds: "Fifty percent of all weapons produced in the world go to the Middle East, which now has the highest per capita expenditure for armaments in the entire world."

We have over-supplied Israel with money and weapons—making a country of about three million Jews a bigger military giant than either Germany, England or France—and more powerful than all the 21 Arab countries combined, with their 150 million people.

In addition to its vast arsenal of the latest conventional U.S. war weapons, Israel in 1986 and for perhaps two decades previously, was the only country in the Middle East to have nuclear weapons. "Since 1965, when Israel began obtaining the required materials and technology from the United States, Israel has built nuclear weapons, configured as missile warheads or as bombs to be dropped from jet aircraft," Stephen Green, author of *Taking Sides*, told me in an interview. He adds:

"In 1965, Israeli loyalists took over 752 pounds of uranium—almost enough to make 38 Hiroshima-sized atomic bombs—from the Nuclear Materials and Equipment Corporation in Apollo, Pennsylvania. Zalman Shapiro, a scientist who once headed the plant, was also a half-owner with the Israeli government of Isorad, an Israeli-based company that made nuclear equipment."

A CIA report released in 1968 confirmed Israel's nuclear capability and stated Tel Aviv was able to develop nuclear devices without publicity. The CIA report also estimated that Israel possessed between 12 and 20 nuclear bombs.

From 1980 to 1982, a California businessman illegally exported to Israel 15 shipments of military timing devices called krytrons that can be used as triggers in nuclear weapons. News reports on May 16, 1985 said a Los Angeles federal grand jury indicted the businessman. The businessman, who mysteriously disappeared, allegedly made transfers from Milco International in California to the Tel Aviv-based Heli Trading Company.

From the beginning of its nuclear development, Israel has refused to join either the non-proliferation pact, or any of the international organizations designed to impose a modicum of safety and sanity on the international race towards genocidal weapons.

As supplier of Israel's war weapons, the United States in one way or another has become embroiled in all of Israel's wars—in 1956, 1967, 1973 and 1982.

In the 1973 Israel-Arab war, Nixon and Kissinger ordered a worldwide nuclear alert to the third stage of nuclear readiness, bringing us two steps away from Armageddon. Furthermore, in the early stages of that war, Israel threatened to use nuclear weapons, and in fact prepared to do so, in order to compel the U.S. to provide "a massive shipment of conventional weapons to Israel," reports a noted American Jew at Massachusetts Institute of Technology, Professor Noam Chomsky. In *The Fateful Triangle: The United States, Israel and the Palestinians*, Chomsky writes:

"The threat was directed at the United States: The Israeli signals would make it clear to the decision-makers in the White House, the Pentagon and the State Department that any more delays might bring catastrophe to the Middle East . . . It may also be surmised that Israeli nuclear-tipped missiles that can reach southern Russia are not really intended to deter the U.S.S.R. but rather to put U.S. planners on notice, once again, that pressures on Israel to accede to a political settlement may lead to a violent reaction . . . with a probability of global nuclear war."

Israel's "secret weapon" against the United States in particular and the West in general, writes Dr. Chomsky, is that, it may act as a "wild country, dangerous to its surroundings, not normal, quite capable of burning the oil fields or even starting a nuclear war."

Israeli use of veiled threats to unleash doomsday on the world has been recognized within Israel. Yaakov Sharett writes in the Israeli *Davar* (November 3, 1982) that the greatest danger facing

Israel today is the "collective version" of Samson's revenge against the Philistines—"Let me perish with the Philistines"—as he brought down the temple in ruins. And he quotes former Defense Minister Pinhas Lavon as saying, "We will go crazy" ("nishtagea") if crossed. Sharett also quotes Labor Party official David Hacohen, who after the Israeli 1967 attack on Egypt, warned, "We have nothing to lose so it is better that we go crazy; the world will know to what a level we have reached." This modern-day "Samson complex" is reinforced by the feeling that "the whole world is against us" because of its ineradicable anti-semitism, a paranoid vision that owes not a little to the belief system of Christian Zionists.

The extremists among the Israeli Jews are still not a majority, and the Christian extremists are still not a majority. However, I have attempted to show that the alliance between these right-wing, militaristic groups gives both a quantum leap in real, unsentimental power and might. Moreover, leaders in both groups are obsessed with their own belief system, their own ideology, their own certitude that they have both the right and the power to help orchestrate not only their own End of Times, but doomsday for the rest of the species.

In 1985, we Americans observed the 40th anniversary of our having dropped the first atomic bomb. For four decades now, Americans and all peoples of the world have lived under the nuclear shadow. Since Hiroshima, we have built more than enough nuclear weapons to destroy all humankind.

Yet we increasingly are urged to build more bombs and spend trillions of dollars in outer space "to keep the peace." Assuming that American nuclear weapons are peace-keepers, does it follow that the peace will be better kept if all the nations of the world become nuclear superpowers?

Somehow in all the sermons of Jerry Falwell and other TV evangelists, I miss their telling us about the Sermon on the Mount. And I miss their reminding us that Christ possessed a way that was not based on military strength. His way was not to obliterate property and people for the sake of a temporary political kingdom on earth. Rather, He came to advance and enhance life. He came with a message of peace. With peace He taught that we might have life—and have it abundantly.

Index

202   INDEX

Nazis, 26, 83, 97, 115, 116, 132
Neoconservative politics, 158, 163, 165, 167
Netanyahu, Benjamin, 138–139
Netanyahu, Benzoin, 191
New Christian Right, 8, 41, 67, 76, 152,
    158, 159, 161, 162, 163, 165, 167,
    168, 180
  and Israeli Right, 158, 159, 162, 164
New Conservatives, The (Howe, Rosenberg),
    159
New York Theological Seminary, 11
New York Times, 11, 12, 47, 76
  and CBS poll, 10
Newsweek, 12
Nielsen survey, 11, 12
Nile River, 83, 141
Nixon, Richard, 76, 199
Non-proliferation pact, 199
Norris, J. Frank, 197
Nuclear Battlefields (Arkin, Fieldhouse), 50
Nuclear holocaust (war), 4, 10, 11, 14, 15,
    17, 25, 26, 27, 28, 30, 33, 34, 39, 40,
    41, 45, 47, 48, 61, 94, 100, 113, 177,
    195, 197, 199
"Nuclear War and the Second Coming of
    Jesus Christ" (Falwell), 35
Nuclear weapons, development of, 50, 147,
    155, 159, 197, 198, 199, 200
  facilities for, 50

Oil, 33
Old Testament, 54, 61, 91, 97, 105, 134,
    135, 168
Old Time Gospel Hour, 12, 21, 32, 33
  See also Falwell, Jerry.
Orientals, 23, 29, 83, 145
Orwell, George, 141
Otis, George, 42–43, 45, 46
Ottoman Empire, 136
Owen, 8–9, 88, 90–92, 95

Palestine, 4, 54, 53, 54, 55, 65, 73, 75, 83,
    84, 86, 96, 97, 124, 133, 134, 135,
    136, 137, 138, 140, 141, 142, 176, 177
  British in, 97, 135–137, 162, 194
  creation of state of, 153

partition of, 176, 185
Palestinian-Israeli conflict, 58, 152, 153,
    168–169
Palestine Liberation Organization (PLO), 85,
    148, 158
Palestinians, 51–58, 62, 64, 65, 67, 75, 85,
    90, 107, 109, 114, 124, 125, 126, 127,
    136, 145, 146, 148, 149, 153, 165,
    168, 169, 173, 175, 176, 194
  Christian, situation of, 127–128
Palmerton, Lord, 136
Parker, Margaret, 185, 188
Peace, 15, 16, 26, 33
Peace Corps, 149
Pentagon, 9, 47, 73
Pentecostal. See Assemblies of God.
Pentecostal Holiness Church, 12, 14
People-to-People, 149
Percy, Charles, 164–165
Peres, Shimon, 121, 191
Perlmutter, Nathan, 154–155
Persia, 16, 33
  See also Iran.
Persians, 53
Peter, 30, 61, 121
Petra, 31
Phalangists, 76
Philadelphia College of the Bible, 15
Phillips, Howard, 76
Pilgrims, 84
Poland, 83
Porat, Hanan, 142
Praise the Lord (PTL), 12, 47
Prayer Breakfast for Israel, 29, 181
Prayer in school, 147, 155, 156
Presbyterians, 147, 148, 152
Price, James, 71–77
Pro-Israel lobby, 163, 164, 165, 166, 167,
    180
Prophecy, 7, 29, 32, 33, 36, 42, 43, 46, 47,
    49, 61, 66, 85, 114, 134, 139, 179, 198
Prophets, 36, 46, 48, 160
Protestants, 137, 147, 148, 153
  early, 134–135, 137
Put, 16
  See also Libya.

Quakers, 152

210

INDEX